40 YEARS
AT THE HOME
OF THE
HOME
HEISMAN

A BOY, A BALL, AND HIS DREAM

RUDY J. RISKA

JOHN S. CLARK

PETER J. CLARK

COACHES CHOICE™

ISBN: 1-58518-523-X
Library of Congress Catalog Card Number: 2001096043

Interior design and layout: Scot Muncaster and Jennifer Bokelmann
Cover design: Rebecca Gold

Coaches Choice
P.O. Box 1828
Monterey, CA 93942
http://www.coacheschoiceweb.com

Heisman Memorial Trophy and likeness of the actual trophy are registered service marks by the Downtown Athletic Club under registration numbers 936,853 and 935,852 respectively.

DEDICATION

To all those whose lives have been touched in some form by Rudy Riska, for your help and willingness to share great stories with the authors and the public. To the Heisman winners, thank you for allowing us a glimpse into your fraternity.

On my twenty-fifth anniversary with the DAC, Club member and former president, Bill Blum, and other friends honored me with a special night. Last year, a similar group of members and friends (coordinated by my assistant Sean Ingram), honored me again—this time for my fortieth anniversary. On both occasions, many Heisman winners, sports celebrities and close friends, had many nice things to say about their relationship and experiences with the DAC and me over the years. Both events provided me with two wonderful, special times to look back on and cherish.

ACKNOWLEDGMENTS

If I tried to list all of those wonderful people whom I would like to recognize, we would need another book. And, I would surely leave out someone special. But, I need to recognize and offer a "very special thank you" to the following:

My wife Lorraine, who together we celebrate 40 years of marriage;

My brother, Steve, who shares my passion for the great game of golf. During our get-togethers, we often talk about how far we have come and how many good friends and associates we have who have given us so much support, encouragement, and respect over the years;

My two special daughters, Elizabeth and Barbara, and our four grandchildren; Brian, Emma, Jessica and Kristin;

ME AND MY INVALUABLE ASSISTANT SEAN INGRAM.

Our mother, who sacrificed so much for us and taught us to always help those less fortunate than others, and to know right from wrong;

Our boyhood friends who we battled with in the various sport competitions, and helped our love for the sports grow;

The New York Yankees organization, for making my dream (also my brother's, who had three years in the organization) a reality, and also for providing four years of experience, memories and friendships;

Reverend Charles Keil and the "Five Points Mission" who provided so many with guidance and comfort, and who gave a young man confidence and respect;

The Downtown Athletic Club and its many members and fellow employees who supported, encouraged and contributed in so many ways to making the past 40 years so enjoyable and successful;

Marge Koenig for her dedication and loyalty;

Bernadette Beglane, for charting new ways and being a complete joy to be around;

Sean Ingram, who is my right arm. He does not receive his due credit for his intelligent and creative work;

John Ott (who started my career at the club), Jim White, Henry Sampers, Tony Tuccillo, Charlie Reynolds and the handball club members;

The fellowship and joy of coaching the championship basketball team and its players;

West Pointer's, Sue and Jim Peterson, along with Major Art Johnson and Colonel Al Rushatz, for those great times on the "Plains";

All of the sports greats (many of whom were my heroes) who were always supportive and available for the many charities and programs;

That special award, The Heisman Trophy, and those special winners who have allowed me into their special fraternity, and who have given me their respect, trust and support over the years;

Arthur Corr and Chuck Benson for their skill with a camera and for contributing to the Club and its programs; and,

Peter and John Clark for believing my forty years would make a book, and giving me an opportunity to look back and enjoy.

To all, a very special thank you.

—Rudy J. Riska

SCOUTING TWO OF THE NEXT GREAT NEW YORK ATHLETES, MY GRANDCHILDREN, BRIAN AND EMMA.

We wish to thank Dr. Jim Peterson and Coaches Choice—Jim we couldn't have done it without you. Terry Neutz Hayden who served as a sounding board throughout—you are the best. Scot Muncaster and Jennifer Bokelmann for their great layout and design work. When called on for widely varying reasons, so many individuals enthusiastically responded with their assistance and input with this project including Cassie Arner, Sean Ingram, Bret Kroencke and Kris Hanson… John DiSomma, Pete Dawkins, Jim Plunkett and Don Friday… Erich Bacher, Dicky Kasson, Randy Wievel and all the others we may be overlooking, but whose efforts are certainly much appreciated. And finally, to our parents for their continued support and whose love of sports has been passed on to their two youngest sons.

—John S. Clark and Peter J. Clark

CONTENTS

ACKNOWLEDGMENTS 4

FOREWORDS 9

INTRODUCTION 13

THE EARLY YEARS 17

THE DOWNTOWN ATHLETIC CLUB 23

A BRIEF HISTORY OF THE DAC 29

THE SPECIAL EVENTS 35

ALL-SPORTS NIGHT 41

HOLLYWOOD AT THE DAC 57

FOOTBALL ROUNDUP EXEMPLARY 61
PLAYER AWARDS DINNER

SALUTE TO BOXING GREATS 73

PRESIDENT'S COUNCIL ON 79
PHYSICAL FITNESS

THE HEISMAN TROPHY 87

WHAT THE HEISMAN MEANT TO ME 117

"Rudy Riska is the best friend the Heisman Trophy has ever had. The guy has contributed so much to the growth of the Heisman, while retaining the strength and meaning of the award. Fans of college football and the Heisman Trophy owe him a debt of gratitude."

—*Chris Fowler*
ESPN College Football Analyst

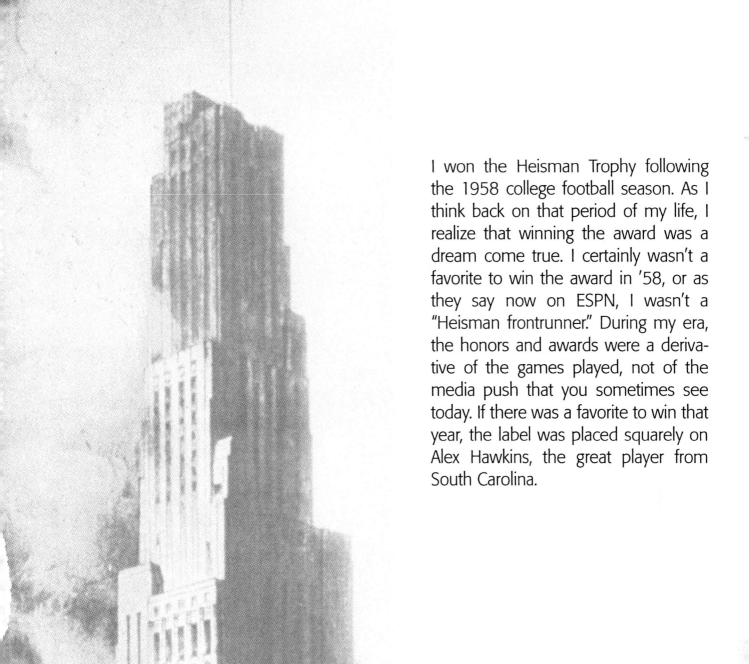

I won the Heisman Trophy following the 1958 college football season. As I think back on that period of my life, I realize that winning the award was a dream come true. I certainly wasn't a favorite to win the award in '58, or as they say now on ESPN, I wasn't a "Heisman frontrunner." During my era, the honors and awards were a derivative of the games played, not of the media push that you sometimes see today. If there was a favorite to win that year, the label was placed squarely on Alex Hawkins, the great player from South Carolina.

FOREWORDS

PETE DAWKINS,
1958 HEISMAN TROPHY WINNER

In an early season win against South Carolina, I was fortunate enough to score four touchdowns for Army, which served as a launching pad for my Heisman bid. As the season progressed, unheralded Army became a Cinderella team on our way to an undefeated season. Even as our successful season was unfolding, I had doubts about winning the Heisman because to me it was a dream… something every college football player greatly desired, but something that was difficult to imagine. Coach Red Blaik also did a pretty good job of keeping us focused on the task at hand, never letting us rest on our laurels.

When I was told that I had indeed won the award, it was a bit overwhelming. Everything happened so fast, it was like I was on a rocket. I was just a young kid from Royal Oak, Michigan, who all of a sudden was the focus of incredible attention. I will always remember the way the folks at the Downtown Athletic Club made my parents feel so special. This was a life event for them, since neither had ever been to New York City, much less ridden in a limousine. From the president of the DAC meeting them at LaGuardia to my mother shopping in the world-class stores of New York to our attending a Broadway show, their royal treatment has been indelibly etched in their minds. As I stood on the stage that evening holding the trophy, I finally realized that it wasn't a dream, it had actually happened. I had won the Heisman Trophy.

One of the great honors Heisman winners enjoy is being invited back each year to the awards dinner and festivities. Through the years, all of the past winners have grown by association with one another, and that is hard to do. There are a lot of ways life tends to pull you apart. Whenever we seemed to get a little bit tattered, there was always one guy there to pull the strings back together—Rudy Riska. Rudy has single-handedly knit together the fabric of the fraternity of Heisman Trophy winners. For 40 years, Rudy has worked tirelessly, though the road hasn't always been smooth for the Heisman or the DAC. Over the years, we have gone through trials and tribulations with the Heisman, but through it all, the one solid rock we could always depend on never let us down.

To me, achievement is a function of effort over time. It is not just effort, and it is not just being there a long time. It is putting the effort in over a long period of time. Rudy Riska epitomizes this. It has been my experience that no matter what I have been involved in over the years, there are always a lot of people whose contributions are important. But within the events that are really successful and truly special, there is always one individual person who has the spirit, the soul, the passion, the commitment, and the belief in what it is all about who will not allow it to be anything but great. For me, and I think for all Heisman winners, Rudy has been that individual with the Heisman, and for that we will forever be grateful. Rudy Riska truly is the spirit and the soul of the Heisman Trophy.

—Pete Dawkins

I received the Heisman Trophy in 1970. This was the beginning of a special relationship with other past winners and with winners yet to come. Yet, as unique of an experience being a Heisman Trophy winner has been, what I cherish most about my association with the Heisman is my relationship with Rudy Riska. Over the past thirty years, Rudy and I

JIM PLUNKETT, 1970 HEISMAN TROPHY WINNER.

have become friends: a friendship that has transcended the Heisman Trophy. We keep in touch by phone and get together every so often at the Heisman Presentation, Heisman Golf Tournaments, or when he gets out to my part of the country, the West Coast. What is special about Rudy is that he is genuinely concerned about the Heisman winners as people. This is evident in conversations with Rudy which center on family, friends and health, not just Heisman-related topics.

I admire Rudy as a man who puts other things aside when it comes to the Heisman Trophy. He helps organize the event, deals with the candidates and the recipients (which is not always easy), and year after year puts on the first-class Heisman Presentation. The one thing that Rudy cares the most about is maintaining the 'integrity' of the Heisman Trophy, making sure it stands alone as the top award of college football. In that regard, he has certainly done an outstanding job.

Our friendship started in 1970. I can remember Rudy taking me under his wing in the Big Apple and showing me the ropes. Back in those days, he would take my friends and me to dinner, the theater and out on the town. I didn't own a tuxedo so he made sure I got one! Those are just some of the things he did to help you feel comfortable and a part of the Heisman family. Some of that has changed today, but Rudy does whatever he can to make sure the Heisman continues in that tradition that has made it so great.

Although people have come and gone at the Heisman, and the Heisman has grown so much in national attention and recognition, the one constant throughout the years has been Rudy Riska. His attention to detail and the effort he expends in promoting the Heisman award and its winners has truly made it a very special fraternity. My hat is off to Rudy—as a friend and as a keeper of the Heisman flame.

—Jim Plunkett

Students of history often marvel at the inner machinations that are unknown to the general public, but necessary for a singular event to occur. The world of sports is no exception. Behind every championship season or game is a myriad of people influencing its outcome in various ways. Whether it is the inspirational figure providing drive to the accomplishment or the organizer who made it possible, the event would not have been the same without their efforts.

INTRODUCTION

Even more interesting than the identity of these people is the relationship they have with the principal figures. At some time or another, most of us have wanted to be "on the inside," a term used to refer to the small circle of elite in a particular area of society, yet very few of us have been fortunate enough to experience this status. This book is about a man who has—Rudy Riska. It is also a chronicle of Rudy's forty-year journey through the "inside" of the sports world.

As you will see in the following photos, stories, and remembrances relating to Rudy Riska's life, you would not be too far askew to say there is an almost Forrest Gump-like attraction for famous figures and Rudy. Over the years, events in Rudy's life have criss-crossed with personalities who had already, or would in the future, make their mark on the sporting world.

Rudy has always been close to the Downtown Athletic Club. In fact, he was born just across the street from the Club. To be precise, he began his long and successful association with the DAC in October 1960. Rudy was (and still is) a natural athlete, who excelled in a number of sports, all of which he engaged in with a zest for competition and a desire to improve. He was with the New York Yankee organization from 1954 through 1958. After he left baseball, he quickly established himself at the Club, developing a host of popular new programs, even as he updated the athletic facilities.

OVER THE YEARS, EVENTS IN RUDY'S LIFE HAVE CRISSCROSSED WITH PERSONALITIES WHO HAD ALREADY, OR WOULD IN THE FUTURE, MAKE THEIR MARK ON THE SPORTING WORLD.

Rudy's first success came with the Club's championship basketball teams of 1962 and 1963, which posted standout records against some of the best amateur competition along the Eastern seaboard. This success led to the start of the Wall Street League and its popular awards dinner and dance. Rudy also instituted volleyball leagues and a handball club and added other activities, such as the West Point competitions and numerous social events.

A highlight of Rudy's time at the DAC has been the growth of the DAC's fitness center and its sports medicine programs, featuring health and wellness seminars, personalized fitness screening and testing, and instructional clinics in a variety of exercise-related areas. For swimmers, Rudy instituted the 100 Mile Club and added both the "swim down the Mississippi" and the "swim around Manhattan" programs. Rudy's efforts were not, however, focused solely on Club members. He instituted the highly successful Saturday morning sports program for children of Club members. This program featured a variety of events that were associated with the President's Council on Physical Fitness.

In addition to the programs Rudy established within the DAC, Rudy was instrumental in creating and maintaining a strong rapport with leading athletic, educational and community organizations, including the Amateur Athletic Union; the National Collegiate Athletic Directors Association; the President's Council on Physical Fitness and Sports; the West Point Athletic Association; the Boys Club of New York; the Atlantic Collegiate Baseball Scouts; the Boxing, Basketball and Football Writers Associations; the Junior Olympics; the New York Police and Fire Department Sports; the National Collegiate Boxing Association; the Howe Cup of Women's Squash; the Women's Sports Foundation; the Golden Spike Award of Collegiate Baseball; the Eastman Kodak Basketball Award; the Touchdown Club of New York; St. John's University; and many, many others.

Rudy has also represented the DAC at many charities, including the Diabetes Foundation; the Red Cross; the Leukemia Foundation; the Police and Fire Widows and Children's Fund and Burn Center; the Make-a-Wish Foundation®; and the U.S. Marine Corps Charity Drives. Furthermore, his dedication to both the DAC programs and his charitable involvement remain as strong today as when he first came to the club.

Forty years later, Rudy remains the cornerstone of the DAC. Over that time, he has come into contact with celebrities and heroes, instituted programs to help various charities, and pursued his passion of a life filled with sport. The following pages provide a glimpse into the life of one of America's great behind-the-scenes sport figures. As you read, you will meet some of the most storied American athletes of the twentieth century. Collectively, the anecdotes present a composite picture of the man who many consider to be the Downtown Athletic Club—Rudy Riska. Despite the extensive and on-going contact with celebrities, Rudy still adheres to the basic principles he learned on the streets of New York City's lower east side. At heart, he remains a boy with a ball and a dream.

—John S. Clark and Peter J. Clark

"I've watched Rudy through the years as a friend and as a person who enjoys seeing things done in a precise manner. One time at a dinner I got up on the dais to say some things about Rudy. The first words that came to me were Joe DiMaggio. Joe DiMaggio did things effortlessly… he had class. It made me think of Rudy Riska. Rudy makes things look easy. He stays in the background and performs effortlessly and beautifully. Rudy Riska is Joe DiMaggio."

—Bill Gallo
New York Daily News

I was born in August, 1936, in the shadow of the Downtown Athletic Club on Greenwich Street. That same year, the legendary coach John Heisman, who was the first Athletic Director at the DAC, passed away. Twenty-four years later, I would begin a forty-year association with the Club.

I grew up on the lower east side of New York, in a neighborhood bordering Little Italy and Chinatown. This is the same area where the famous Governor Al Smith and celebrities Eddie Cantor and Jimmy Durante came from. I have loved sports ever since I can remember. During the 1940's, the organized teams and facilities that are so prevalent today were a rarity, so our sports centered around the all-purpose "Spaldeen" ball. Among the games that used this ball were stickball, punch ball, stoop ball, and handball, each with their own variations depending upon where you lived. Each neighborhood had its own "playing fields." The fields on which I played were on Henry Street near Public School #1. There were very few cars parked on that street, and only one tenement, which kept broken windows to a minimum.

THE
EARLY
YEARS

CHAPTER ONE

I also had my own game I would play against the side of the school's stoop. I would throw the "Spaldeen" against a rounded aperture that, if hit just right, would make the ball fly right back to me. Many nights, I would play this game under the streetlights, imagining that I was pitching for my favorite team, the Giants, against the Giants' hated rival— the Dodgers (many of whom I would later meet and befriend through the Club). The only area to play real baseball was "the lots," a cinder and rock field located under the Manhattan Bridge. The older guys in my neighborhood dominated this space; when we were old enough to play one or two games a year, our equipment was a black-taped baseball and an old broken bat we nailed together so we could play. I guess throwing the heavily taped ball gave me a strong arm, and eventually the chance to live my dream as a professional baseball player. I still see many of the guys from the old neighborhood, and we always retell stories of growing up and competing at sports. It kept most of us out of trouble and gave us lifetime friendships.

THE "SPALDEEN"

Reprinted in part with permission from Steve Jacobson and his article "Back in the Pink" that appeared in *Newsday*, May 9, 1999.

Pieces of Americana have a habit of resurfacing a generation later. What Baby Boomers grew up with is now known to today's hip as "retro." Even professional sport shows evidence of this phenomenon in the designs of new stadiums and arenas. But ask any New Yorker born between the 1940s and the mid 1970s the name of the dominant ball used in the sandlots or city streets, and odds are the answer will be "Spaldeen." Although formal records indicate the 1950s as the first appearance of the Spaldeen, Rudy Riska and his friends were using it in the 1940s. The Spaldeen went on to become a mainstay of playground life all over New York.

If you grew up in New York, including the city and suburbs, you need no identification for the ball or the games. In case you just moved from Mars or Kansas City, the Spaldeen was a hollow rubber ball the color of bubble gum. It was called Spal-DEEN because the manufacturer stamped it Spalding, and that's how we said it.

The Spaldeen had limitless possible uses. If you had the ball in your pocket, you could make up a game to play with your sister or little brother while you were out with your parents. You could even create a game with half a broken Spaldeen. Spalding sold millions of them, mostly in the Northeast from the early '50s until 1978, and there's a memory for each. Most games included climbing a fence or probing a sewer to get the ball back.

Originally, it came from rejects and leftovers from the making of tennis balls—before they put the fur on. You know, like chicken wings used to get thrown away

Next to our various games with the legendary "Spaldeen" ball, my other youthful passion was basketball. I thank God for such recreation centers as the Riis House, Mariner's Temple and the Cherry Street Gym, where my friends and I would spend the cold winter nights playing pick-up games. Marty Glickman's voice as commentator of the Knicks games made me a fan of that team, but while I rooted for that Knicks team of the early '50s, my favorite player wore a different uniform. I was a big fan of the Boston Celtic great Bob Cousy. I attended a New Year's Eve basketball double-header at Madison Square Garden featuring the Rochester Royals against the Indianapolis Olympians in the first game, with the Celtics and Knicks squaring off in the second game. I can still recall that entire evening as if it were yesterday. The highlight of that night was at the end of the Knicks' game. With the Knicks leading by two points with about a minute to go, the Knicks froze the ball. Dick McGuire was dribbling the ball, and it was deflected. Cousy picked up the loose ball and headed toward his basket, but was cut off at half court by Carl Braun.

Cousy used a behind-the-back dribble to get by Braun and moved into the basket for a layup. But just as Cousy was going up, Nat "Sweetwater" Clifton came out of nowhere to block the shot. Cousy pulled the ball down and, while still in the air, went behind his back and dropped a perfect pass over his shoulder to Bill Sharman who made the basket at the buzzer to send the game into overtime. The capacity crowd sat stunned for a moment, then erupted. The whole Garden was talking about that sequence of plays. The Knicks went on to win the game on the strength of Max Zazlolsky's 32 points. On the way home that night and for the next few weeks, my buddies and I tried to emulate Cousy's play.

Fast-forward a number of years to the DAC and the All Sports Night dinner, when we honored Bob Cousy and I first got to meet one of my heroes. Years later at a Heisman Foundation golf outing in Hilton Head, Bob participated, and I got to play in his foursome along with Don Criqui. Bob's same mystique came through on the golf course, and

until the Anchor Bar in Buffalo created a desirable snack food.

Stores would get Spaldeens by the box, and the slick ones of us could reach in and pick out the firm ones from among the soft ones, somewhat like finding good peaches. When Spalding stopped making them, they were 25 cents each. They had a special aroma, somewhat like the bouquet of the bubble gum that used to be packed with baseball cards.

Some people recall the Spaldeen as the second implement of stickball: Rule 1. Steal one broom, and snap off the stick. Hit the ball and run the bases. First is at the right curb, second is the manhole cover in the middle of the street, and so on. If the batted ball was hindered by a wire or garbage can or redirected into the bushes by a moving car, it was a hindu. We learned the art of compromising disputes with do-overs.

The "Spaldeen" Facts
Official Name: *Spalding High-Bounce ball*
Correct Pronunciation: *spal-DEEN*
Distinguishing Characteristics: *pink color, rough texture, rubbery smell*
First issued: *1949*
Last year produced: *1979*
Games played with ball: *Stickball, hit the penny, box baseball, stoopball, punch ball*
Price in 1959: *25 cents*

Don and I were just fascinated by it all.

I attended Metropolitan High School and made the baseball team my first year. This was the first time I played in an organized baseball game on real grass fields with umpires and uniforms. I was an outfielder that first year, and after a rough start, I ended up playing pretty well. My second year, I did not go out for the team. Like a lot of other kids in that era, I worked after school and couldn't find time to play baseball. Plus, I was crazy about basketball then, and would play half-court games every evening when I got home from work. Going into my senior year of high school, a few of my school's baseball players asked me to play, since they needed a pitcher and remembered my strong arm. I worked it out with my boss so that when we had games, somebody would cover for me. I had never pitched in a real game before, and as can be expected, I was terrible in the beginning. But once the league games started, I began to do well.

A big game that really stands out in my mind was when my high school was celebrating Field Day. On this day, the entire school would report to a park instead of school. There would be all sorts of races and activities between individual students and whole

ONE OF MY CHILDHOOD HEROES, BOB COUSY, THE NIGHT HE RECEIVED THE ROBERT STEWART AWARD. CASEY CONRAD, EXECUTIVE DIRECTOR OF THE PRESIDENT'S COUNCIL ON PHYSICAL FITNESS AND SPORTS, AND ERNIE FRANK, THE ALL-SPORTS DINNER CHAIRMAN, PRESENT COUSY WITH HIS PORTRAIT.

ME AS A YOUNG MINOR LEAGUER

classes. Our baseball team was scheduled to play George Washington High, a perennial championship team, at Babe Ruth Stadium, which was located across from Yankee Stadium. It all came together for me that day. I pitched a no-hitter, and a Yankee scout by the name of Paul Krichell was in attendance. He was the same scout who had signed Lou Gehrig. He invited me to a tryout at Yankee Stadium after I graduated in June. At the tryout, I did well and was invited back for a final looksee; however, I was obligated to be a camp counselor at the Five Points Mission Church's summer camp in Cornwall-on-the-Hudson. The Five Points Mission Church and facilities were a God-send to so many people in my neighborhood. It was a Methodist Church with a kindergarten school, Sunday school and gymnasium. They offered free movies on Friday nights during the winter, Christmas gifts, food for the needy and the opportunity for two weeks at camp in the summer. They had three sessions of two-week groups. The church's minister Dr. Charles Keil, befriended me and my family and gave me the opportunity to be one of the boy's counselors even though I had no prior experience. His confidence in me was a big boost at an important time in my life, and I wasn't about to let him down. *(In fact, in over forty years at the Downtown Athletic Club, there have been many, many people who have given me a helping hand for which I am most grateful and I often remind myself of their kindness.)* I subsequently explained my situation to the Yankees, and they agreed to contact me after the summer job was over.

Following my stint as a counselor, the Yankees invited me back for their September tryouts featuring the best prospects in the tri-state area. I guess the summer camp work and nature had taken its effect. I had grown a few inches and filled out my previously skinny frame. I was so strong, I could see the impression I was making on the Yankee scout who was catching me. In the tryout, I was to pitch two innings. But, I struck out all six batters, so they asked me to pitch one more inning. I struck out three more. In the clubhouse after the scrimmage, I met Mickey Rendine, the Yankees' clubhouse man. Mickey looked after me, and we became friends. (Mickey just recently retired after a long career with the Jets and Yankees.) Mickey said he heard I was going to be offered a contract. I could not believe it! Even today, over forty-seven years later, the entire experience is so vivid in my memory.

HERE I AM AS A MEMBER OF THE KINGSPORT, TENNESSEE MINOR LEAGUE TEAM. MY MANAGER IN KINGSPORT WAS THE LEGENDARY LEO "MUSCLES" SHOALS.

Sure enough, a few days later, my father came to a park near our home to find me because the Yankee scout sent to sign me, Harry Hess, was in our apartment with a contract. I signed for a small bonus and was to report the next season at St. Joseph in the Class C Western League. However, before spring training, the league folded, and I was subsequently assigned to Monroe of the Louisiana State League. I never got to Hattiesburg, Mississippi, for spring training. Instead, I was reassigned to Statesboro, an independent team in the Georgia State League. What an experience, and what a waste of time being a green rookie. I was overlooked by the manager at Statesboro who was only interested in veterans. Nobody worked with me or helped me learn the ropes of minor-league life. After three weeks, I was sent to Bristol in the Appalachian League—a Yankee farm team. When I got to Bristol, three days before the start of the 1955 season, the manager, Dave Madison (who would later become a friend and supporter), gave me the news that I was being assigned to Kingsport, an independent team in the same league.

So, with five teams and no innings pitched to my credit, I arrived in Kingsport, Tennessee, where I would pitch the entire season. My manager was legendary minor-league home run hitter, Leo "Muscles" Shoals. I was still wide-eyed after two days with the team, when I was further amazed by being selected to pitch the home opener. Who knows what Leo (or for that fact my fellow pitchers) was thinking! I lasted six innings in the opener and earned the win. Crazy! I would go on to win twelve games against eight losses. More importantly, however, the experience of spending six months away from home really changed me.

I really came of age during my four-and-one-half years with the Yankee organization and my one year with the Orioles organization. These times have a lasting and cherished spot in my memories. The quest to make it to the big leagues, teammates who I have stayed in touch with throughout the years, and managers and friends like Ken Silvestri, Randy Gumpert, and Lee MacPhail, were all part of a very magical time for me. My brother Steve, who would sign with the Yankees in 1960 and would spend three years playing in the Yankee farm system, has the same wonderful memories from those experiences.

Unfortunately, my dream ended with an injury to my pitching arm. Chronic bursitis to my elbow was the diagnosis. Without the injury, could I have pitched in the majors? I believe so, but it was a different time and many circumstances made the road to the majors difficult for me. However, those years and experiences prepared me for my next role in life.

MY BROTHER STEVE AND NEW YORK YANKEE GREAT, DON MATTINGLY. STEVE AND I ARE BOTH VERY PROUD TO SAY WE PLAYED IN THE YANKEE FARM SYSTEM FOR A NUMBER OF YEARS.

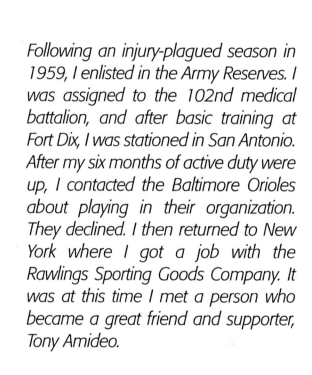

Following an injury-plagued season in 1959, I enlisted in the Army Reserves. I was assigned to the 102nd medical battalion, and after basic training at Fort Dix, I was stationed in San Antonio. After my six months of active duty were up, I contacted the Baltimore Orioles about playing in their organization. They declined. I then returned to New York where I got a job with the Rawlings Sporting Goods Company. It was at this time I met a person who became a great friend and supporter, Tony Amideo.

The
DOWNTOWN
ATHLETIC CLUB

CHAPTER TWO

MY BROTHER, STEVE, WITH THE MAN
RESPONSIBLE FOR GETTING ME MY
FIRST JOB AT THE DAC, TONY AMIDEO.

Tony Amideo ran one of the pre-eminent sporting goods establishments on Nassau Street in Manhattan. Ironically, calling on Tony as a Rawlings representative was not the first time I had met him. As I mentioned before, my friends and I didn't have the greatest equipment to play baseball with. We had gotten tired of taping up balls and nailing together bats, so we decided to pool our money to buy a real bat. We managed to scrape up a whopping total of 50 cents, and made the trek to Amideo's store. We asked Tony if we would be able to get a bat with the money we had. Tony led us to a barrel of defective bats and pulled one out that was shaped like a bow. Understandably, we questioned Amideo about the bat's awkward shape, to which he replied, "This bat is used for hitting curve balls." Well, we had never seen a curve ball, and didn't know that Amideo was joking. So, I thanked him, bought the bat and made the twenty-five minute walk back to our field. I was the first one to try out the "curve-ball bat." The pitcher didn't throw a curve ball, and none of us had any success at the plate. After a short, futile batting practice, we headed back to Amideo's store where Tony was waiting expectantly. We said, "Tony, the bat you sold us doesn't work. You can't hit a curve ball with it." Amideo responded, "Well, how are you holding it?" We showed him how we held the bat with the bow facing outwards toward the pitcher. Tony watched our demonstration and said, "No wonder you aren't hitting anything. You have to have the bow on the inside." So, back we went to our field to try again, only to be met with the same results. Finally, after two hours of marching back and forth to Nassau Street, Amideo let us in on the joke. But for our troubles, he gave us a real bat to use.

When I called on Tony as a Rawling's representative, he asked me if I wanted to make some extra money in the evenings while staying in shape. The Downtown Athletic Club was looking for someone to run its basketball program. I was familiar with the Club because I had played basketball against the Club team. I also remembered my father taking my brother and me into the lobby of the Club to see the Heisman Trophy. I still recall the last name engraved on the trophy—Glenn Davis, West Point, 1946. Later that year, I went to the movie *The Spirit of West Point,* featuring "Doc" Blanchard and Glenn Davis. In the process, I became a lifetime fan of those two great athletes and of West Point. Needless to say, I told Tony that I would love to work at the DAC. A few days later, I was interviewed and given the part-time position of gym instructor.

ONE OF THE GREAT DAC BASKETBALL TEAMS THAT I WAS FORTUNATE ENOUGH TO HAVE THE OPPORTUNITY TO COACH.

DURING MY FORTY YEARS AT THE DAC, I HAVE HAD THE OPPORTUNITY TO
MEET A NUMBER OF EXCEPTIONAL INDIVIDUALS, INCLUDING KEVIN MURPHY
(L), LONGTIME MEMBER OF THE CLUB AND CHAIRMAN OF SEVERAL DAC
SPORTS DINNERS OVER THE YEARS, AND MIKE KRZYZEWSKI (R), THE HIGHLY
SUCCESSFUL HEAD MEN'S BASKETBALL COACH AT DUKE UNIVERSITY.

I fell in love with the job at the DAC from the first day. I remember being in the locker room and striking up a conversation with one of the DAC members. The next day, I
asked the locker room attendant who the individual was, and he answered that the man
was a big-shot on Wall Street. I was amazed that such an important man would treat me
as an equal, much less talk to me at all. I soon realized that all the members acted the
same way. I was a jock, and they were going to be playing sports, so the playing field was
leveled. I was only 24.

During my first weeks on the job at the DAC, I met some wonderful individuals who,
over the years, became very important to my professional development and success.
One of the first men I met was Jim White, a former Notre Dame All-American and captain of the Giants. Jim took the time to talk to me about my background and introduce
me to the other members who used the Club's athletic facilities. (In the late 50s and early
60s, the Downtown Athletic Club was primarily a social and business club for the shipping, banking and Wall Street industries. Maybe five percent of the 4,500 members uti-
lized the athletic activities.)

I began to think of the Club as a career job and in 1962, I was asked to work full-time running the entire department of gymnasium activities. I eagerly said "yes." The only problem was the position's low pay. Naturally, being married with a young daughter (Elizabeth) at home, I was concerned. Members from the handball group stepped forward (John Ott, Henry Sampers, Tom Kennedy, Jim White, Bill Foster, and Charlie Reynolds) and had the Club increase my salary.

The funny thing is, I almost quit a year earlier because of a confrontation with the handball group. The manager requested I run a Club handball tournament, but never informed the committee. When I removed the old tournament sheets, the attendant on the floor angrily questioned my authority. I explained the situation and went back to my office. Around 5:00 p.m. that day, I was called to come to the handball floor where I was confronted by the aforementioned group (all of whom would later become close friends of mine) and told to stay out of the handball courts. Words were exchanged, and I left. Since it was Friday, I went home and told my wife about the incident, half expecting that I would be fired on Monday morning.

The next day, I took my wife and daughter to the Prospect Park Zoo. Suddenly, I noticed that one of the handball members I had words with, John Ott, was walking toward

THE HANDBALL CLUB L-R: JOHN OTT, TOM KENNEDY AND CHARLIE REVTER, ALONG WITH PAUL HORNUNG. THIS GROUP, LED BY JOHN OTT, WAS INSTRUMENTAL IN GETTING MANY OF THE PROGRAMS I IMPLEMENTED OFF OF THE GROUND.

us. (Later I learned that Ott, who would become President of the DAC, was a walker and would walk from downtown Brooklyn out to Prospect Park.) I said to my wife, "Let's get away from him," but it was too late. Ott walked right over to us. I introduced my family, and we exchanged pleasantries as if nothing had happened the day before. After we parted, my wife remarked that Ott seemed like a nice man, but I told her he was one of the individuals from the night before who had complained.

I went to work the following Monday, not knowing what to expect. When I arrived in my office, my phone rang, and I was directed to go down to the handball courts. The group from the previous Friday was waiting for me. This time, however, they were friendly and encouraged me to run the handball program as I saw fit. The handball group would eventually grow to over a hundred members and form the handball club, the backbone of many successful events I helped to establish at the DAC. Their friendship, respect and support enabled me to accomplish what I did.

I developed the Wall Street basketball league with an annual awards dinner; a noon-time volleyball league; and the handball club with its various competitions and dinner. The following year, 1963, the gentleman in charge of the health-services department, John Reggione, and I were appointed to oversee the entire athletic department. John had been with the club for over ten years and felt slighted by not being named sole Athletic Director. However, John was always a friend, and we worked closely together, while establishing a strong athletic program at the DAC. The following year, John was offered an opportunity in the food industry and left the Club. Subsequently, I was appointed Athletic Director at the DAC.

To call the Downtown Athletic Club (DAC) just another gentlemen's club is akin to referring to the pyramids of Egypt as a minor architectural undertaking. The DAC is one of the most storied clubs in New York City history. Its membership rolls and lists of guests who have attended its many events read like a Who's Who of the sporting world, industry and society. The DAC has served its members throughout the twentieth century with athletic leagues and social events, some becoming annual events that draw national and international attention.

A BRIEF HISTORY OF THE DAC

CHAPTER THREE

The DAC was not built on a foundation of long-term success. Like other businesses that weather the passage of time, the DAC has seen its share of adversity. Each challenge, however, has been met with a determination to persevere that has allowed the club to continue operations and serve its members and the community at large.

Credit for the creation of the DAC belongs to two businessmen: James A. Kennard and Philip D. Slinguff. From a conversation the two had on a Los Angeles park bench, they developed an idea that would have a lasting impact on America's sporting culture. The two entrepreneurs were riding high in the late 1920s, due to a healthy economy at the time and wise business investments over the years. Like many others at that time, Kennard and Slinguff were always on the lookout for opportunities to make a large profit in a relatively short amount of time. Having been successful in starting up gentlemen's clubs elsewhere, Kennard and Slinguff developed a plan to open a club in America's business center—Wall Street. The two took stock of the competition in the area and were surprised to find that no other health club existed in the downtown Wall Street area. If the businessmen on Wall Street were so inclined, they would have had to travel uptown to the New York Athletic Club situated adjacent to Central Park. Knowing the demands on these businessmen's time, Kennard and Slinguff astutely surmised that if they could find a suitable location near Wall Street, they could undoubtedly be able to make a small fortune in membership dues from the bankers, stockbrokers and other businessmen.

In 1926, the two DAC founders acted on their idea and began to pre-sell memberships to their club to the area executives, using high-pressure sales tactics to sell the high-priced memberships and drawing criticism from the local press. Undaunted, the pair continued to pound the pavement, altering the price to suit the perspective buyer, all the while collecting a 25% to 30% commission on each membership sold. To make the memberships more appealing, Kennard and Slinguff allowed the lifetime memberships to be transferable, in effect allowing the memberships to be traded like stock. They staged the Club's first official meeting on October 6, 1926, when three officers, as well as two governors, were elected. As revenue from memberships continued to pour in, the organizational structure of the Club began to take shape. Organizational efforts included a site committee to find the most advantageous location for the Club. In 1927, this committee settled on the Club's current location, which at the time was a series of shabby houses. An upper limit of $450,000 was set for the purchase of the real estate, and the committee began negotiations.

On January 26, 1929, the architects presented multiple designs for the board's consideration. One called for a 22-story edifice; the other for a 35-story skyscraper. There seemed to be very little debate: the Club would be a conspicuous part of the famous lower Manhattan skyline, the taller the better. The original plans for the Club underwent a series of modifications over a period of several months, but after the building loan of three million dollars was approved by General Realty and Utilities Corporation (later a neighbor at 21 West Street) on March 12, 1929, construction began. In the meantime, memberships continued to sell, with lifetime memberships reaching a sold-out status by December, 1928. In that same month, a constitutional amendment was passed by the Club that expanded the Board of Governors to 18 men.

Despite the economic depression that ravaged the country, the DAC forged ahead with the creation of its Club structure. The Board hired H.R. Schaufert to manage the Club

at the princely sum of $833.34 a month. The Club also hired an accomplished French chef, Jean Chantrelle. By the end of that year, the Board was actively searching for an Athletic Director. They soon found their man in the renowned football coach John Heisman, who was given a salary of $600 per month and was made a life member. No expense was spared furnishing the Club, despite the gloomy financial situation gripping the rest of the country. In March, 1930, for example, over $56,000 was spent on china. The next month, the DAC applied for membership in the Metropolitan Squash Association, offered foreign consuls non-resident memberships, set room rental rates ($9.00 per day for a suite, $4.00-$5.00 for a single), and approved the budget for its athletic equipment and furnishings. No corners were cut in making the DAC a show-place facility.

In the summer of 1930, auditors were hired, and the bank was selected for payroll. Although progress on the athletic floors was slow, the Club reached a stage of completion sufficient for the first regular meeting of the Board to be held on-site in September, 1930.

So, nearly a year after the Great Depression began, the Club was opened for business. The building itself was imposing, the staff was skilled, the membership was large, and the officers and governors were dedicated. The twelfth-floor pool was an engineering wonder. The view of the Hudson shipping lanes was superb. The cuisine was superior. But, it was all a delusion. Prudent men would have padlocked the doors and declared bankruptcy, since even more money was needed to complete the Club's facilities. As a result, more members were needed for dues income and operating revenue. And suddenly, the Club's initial debt of three million dollars seemed like an insurmountable obstacle.

Gentlemen's clubs in the 1920s and 1930s served to bolster a man's esteem and propagate his social class. Men of society placed great importance on where diplomas were earned (e.g., Harvard, Yale, Princeton, Andover, Exeter, and Groton), whether money was old money or new money, what pedigrees individuals had, and which boards men sat on. Theirs was a closed way of life. At a time when their way of life was threatened, the captains of industry who were members of the DAC fought long and hard to preserve the value and integrity of their Club.

Obviously, this caste system was inequitable, and in many ways intolerable, but it did carry with it a trait that may have saved the Club: loyalty. Once a man had moved to the fringes of this particular vestige of upper class, he adopted its patterns. He wore the appropriate clothing; he maintained the proper ethical standards in private and business life; he gave generously to the appropriate causes; and he was a staunch defender of the status quo. The DAC was at the epicenter of this caste system on Wall Street. Despite its newness, the Club was populated by men devoted to preserving their way of life.

The Club's tenuous financial situation continued through 1937, during which time the Club reorganized as part of a legal settlement from

THE WAY THE CLUB
LOOKED IN 1929.

32

THE POOL, CONSTRUCTED WITH A WELDED-STEEL BOX SUPPORT, WAS NOT ONLY THE HIGH-
EST ELEVATED AQUATICS FACILITY IN THE WORLD IN 1929, BUT WITH ITS 440 TONS OF
WATER, RANKED AS AN ENGINEERING MARVEL.

a bankruptcy declaration. While the Club struggled to pay its debts, a condition facing most businesses, it was viewed as a feasible operation. Despite the fact that some members resigned due to economic hardships, there always seemed to be new members ready to take their place. The repeal of prohibition in 1933 and the new emphasis on athletic pursuits during the 1930s also helped bolster club revenues.

The DAC is well-known for the events it stages today; however, evidence exists of early members organizing similarly successful events. To a great extent, these events were the result of Club members using the occasions as an oasis away from the economic woes facing the country. For example, during the very first year of the Club's operation, a golf outing was held, the popular Fight Night was staged, holiday parties were thrown, exhibitions were set up featuring famous billiards players, and luncheons were held. Even then, famous celebrities were drawn to the DAC, including Jack Dempsey and Grantland Rice.

While the social agenda was taking shape, Heisman, assisted by Bill Bradley and Olympic swimmer Fred Spongberg, developed the athletic programs, many of which survive to this day. The trio organized competitions in handball, squash, basketball, volleyball, badminton and bowling. They also created a "superstar's competition," where contestants had to compete in seven events. Boxing and fencing lessons were provided for club members. Heisman also organized a gridiron club for collegiate football stars. One of the most popular programs set up at this time was the Sons of Members athletic program, beneficiaries of which can be found on the Club roster today.

Heisman used his reputation and status as the Club's director of athletics to emphasize to Club members the importance of adopting a fitness routine. With Heisman's constant exhortations, members began crowding all the important athletic facilities. For example, the squash club averaged 100 players per day, and weight-lifting participants increased sixty percent from 1932 to 1933. The pool, massage tables, and sun terrace were all crowded. The demand was so great that extra gym classes were added in October 1933.

During the 1920s, miniature golf was a fad that swept the nation. However, it never caught on with the membership, and in 1934, the seventh-floor golf course was dismantled. The Club sold the golf clubs for fifty cents each, but this did not stop the Club members from enjoying one-day events on a real golf course—despite the high cost of participation. For example, a day at the Lido Club in Long Beach including golf, a field day, luncheon and a shore dinner cost a person the exorbitant amount of $6.75! During that period, the celebrated Winged Foot Club in Mamaroneck was the site of the DAC's annual President's Tournament, for which Walter Conwell donated a permanent trophy.

THE SKELETON OF THE CLUB RECEIVES A COVERING IN THIS VIEW FROM THE ROOF OF THE WEST STREET DOCKS.

The rejuvenation of the Club, its athletic facility usage, and events during the mid-30s came as the benefit of increased membership. From August 1932 to January 1933, 600 new members enrolled, pushing the Club roster to 3,000. Almost all of these new recruits were "optionals," meaning they paid no dues. But, they kept the Club busy with constant traffic. So driven was the Club to continue acquiring new members that a 1934 Chevrolet was displayed in the lobby to be given away in a drawing when the membership reached the 3,000 mark. In fact, the drive for new members continued through the 1930s and early 1940s until it was capped at 3,250 in 1944 by Club Chairman John Postell, and at 3,700 in 1950 by Wilbur Jurden.

The rescue of the Club by the membership and Board in the 1930s led to a Golden Age of sorts for the Club. Buoyed by the expanded membership, athletic programs and special events continued to be the benchmark of the DAC through the war years up until the present day. That is not to say the Club totally escaped all financial difficulties. In fact, monetary problems plagued the Club during the middle to late 1940s until the membership, led by Board President Wilbur Jurden, undertook a plan to purchase the Club. Through shrewd negotiations and the generosity of the Club members, the DAC membership purchased the clubhouse in May, 1950.

Since that time, the Club has been host to many personalities and exciting events. While no person can foretell what the future holds for the DAC, the history of the Club combined with the dedication of its loyal membership and employees truly makes it a monument to a glorious period in America.

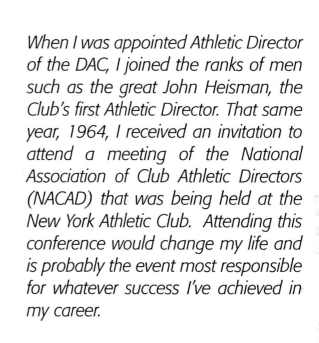

When I was appointed Athletic Director of the DAC, I joined the ranks of men such as the great John Heisman, the Club's first Athletic Director. That same year, 1964, I received an invitation to attend a meeting of the National Association of Club Athletic Directors (NACAD) that was being held at the New York Athletic Club. Attending this conference would change my life and is probably the event most responsible for whatever success I've achieved in my career.

THE SPECIAL EVENTS

CHAPTER FOUR

JAMAAL WILKES, RICHARD "DUKE" LLEWELLYN, JOHN WOODEN, AND
DAVID ROBINSON AT A JOHN WOODEN AWARD DINNER. DUKE LLEWELLYN
WAS INSTRUMENTAL IN THE CREATION OF THIS AWARD AND SERVED AS A
MENTOR TO ME FOR MANY YEARS.

NACAD was made up of 35 athletic directors from the great clubs across the country. These individuals were the best in their fields, with accomplishments and experiences at the highest level. In those five days of meetings, presentations and social gatherings, I was exposed to so many new ideas that I could not wait to get back to the Club and implement them. Subsequently, I became friends with many of the directors; four became lifetime friends, mentors and supporters.

Richard "Duke" Llewellyn of the Los Angeles Athletic Club is a man ahead of his time in club programming, facilities and philosophy. Over the years, Duke has been my mentor and a true friend. We have shared some great times, including attending several conventions together. The NACAD members loved to hear the stories of our adventures together, especially our taking on the great western rivers. Duke was the creative force in the development of the John Wooden Award, named after the great UCLA coach and presented to the college basketball player of the year.

Robert Stewart was the director of the President's Council on Fitness and Sports, and a former athlete at Syracuse University. Bob, along with Stan Musial, would take the

Council to new levels of success. Between 1965 and 1975, fitness became a lifestyle for many people. I was fortunate to have Bob and Stan's guidance and to have them include me in their national program. Bob died at too young an age, but the DAC named a fitness award after him that is presented annually. I often brought Bob's sons and daughter to some of the events.

To this day, Joe Ingrassia and I work together on different projects. Joe has been an athlete, Club governor, Club captain and president of the New York Athletic Club for over 45 years. Joe's contributions to the success of the NYAC are many. His friendship and thoughtful consideration to include me at various NYAC events over the years has been sincerely appreciated.

Ray Lumpp was a member of the 1948 gold-medal, U.S. Olympic basketball team. A former New York Knick and currently Athletic Director at the NYAC, Ray has contributed much to amateur sport in New York City.

The NACAD continues to this day, and I owe a lot to so many members of that exceptional organization for their help and support throughout my career.

Fresh with new ideas that I had gleaned from my first NACAD meetings, I started to develop what would become a series of special dinners that promoted athletics at the club. Over the years, we would be fortunate to honor numerous sport legends, and, in the process, gain their support and participation in charitable causes.

A basketball legend and true New Yorker, Frank McGuire and I first met in 1965, when the DAC basketball team won the St. Anthony's Tournament. Frank would visit the Club (with his friends who were Club members) whenever he was in the city. He was coaching at South Carolina at the time. The St. Anthony's Tournament was held in Frank's boyhood neighborhood. When he heard that we had won the tournament, Frank congratulated me and invited me to join him for dinner, which I was more than excited to do. At this dinner, we were joined by a who's who of basketball. A number of individuals, including Joe Lapchick, Lou Carnesecca, Ben Carnevale, Jack Curran and others, were in attendance.

(L-R) DINNER CHAIRMAN MARK VARRICHIO, JOE TORRE, BILLIE JEAN KING, JERRY APODACA —PRESIDENT'S COUNCIL ON FITNESS & SPORTS, EARL CAMPBELL, AND IRV CROSS. BILLIE JEAN WAS THE RECIPIENT OF THE PRESIDENT'S COUNCIL ON PHYSICAL FITNESS AWARD.

Frank introduced me as a peer, and over the years I became friends with many at that table. I was honored, proud and happy when a few years ago, several of Frank's former players from his undefeated national championship team at North Carolina (Tommy Kearns, Bob Young and Walt O'Hara) formed the Frank McGuire Foundation to honor high school coaches who, like Frank, dedicated themselves to helping young people attain success in society. The dinners and associated programs have been a huge success. They help keep the name and memory of Frank McGuire alive for future generations.

TWO OF HOCKEY'S FINEST PLAYERS EVER — DENIS POTVIN AND MIKE BOSSY.

With the growth of athletic usage at the Club, my responsibilities increased, and I added to the staff. I have been blessed to have some really talented assistants who have made my job so much easier.

Pat Kirby was one of the champion handball players in the country. I asked Pat if he would like to work as my assistant. With the approval of the athletic committee, Pat came aboard. His subsequent contributions to the program were substantial. When Pat moved on to Arizona, a good friend, Vic Colaio, took his place and further added to the success of the athletic department. When Vic eventually left the DAC, Mike Giardina came aboard. During Mike's tenure at the Club, the Club store was expanded and the number of hours of athletic programs offered was increased.

A STAR-STUDDED GROUP OF ATTENDEES AT A STREET AND SMITH'S BASKET-BALL AWARDS DINNER — MIKE NOONE, SATCH SANDERS (BOSTON CELTICS), JOHN ANDARIESE (N.Y. KNICKS ANNOUNCER), SAL SCHILIRO, TOMMY HEINSOHN (BOSTON CELTICS), AND DEAN SMITH (NORTH CAROLINA).

DAC PRESIDENT BILL BLUM WITH HALL OF FAME RUNNING BACK JIM BROWN.

We expanded the DAC's athletics schedule due in large part to the policy change that was enacted in 1976 welcoming women as members. Slowly, the women's membership numbers grew, and women athletes became among the honorees at the various sport dinners. The Saturday morning boys program we ran for members' children became the boys AND girls program. We began to host many women's organizations and competitions, such as the Howe Cup squash championships, the Women's Sports Foundation, and women's strength and body-building events.

Donna deVarona was both an honoree and an emcee at many of these events. Other honorees included Dr. Tenley Albright, Carol Blazejowski, Nancy Lieberman-Cline, Nancy Hogshead, Chamique Holdsclaw, Billy Jean King, Rachel McLish, Shannon Miller, and Mary Lou Retton. They were all outstanding and contributed much to both the membership and the Club overall.

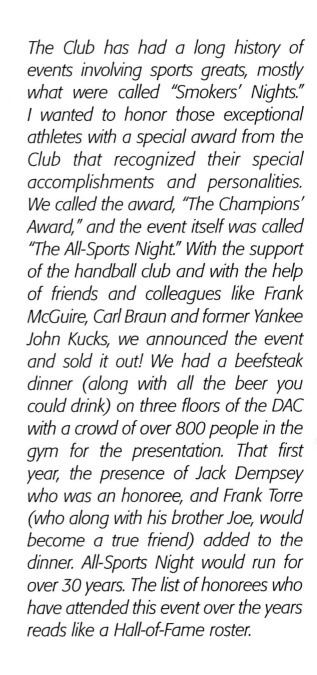

The Club has had a long history of events involving sports greats, mostly what were called "Smokers' Nights." I wanted to honor those exceptional athletes with a special award from the Club that recognized their special accomplishments and personalities. We called the award, "The Champions' Award," and the event itself was called "The All-Sports Night." With the support of the handball club and with the help of friends and colleagues like Frank McGuire, Carl Braun and former Yankee John Kucks, we announced the event and sold it out! We had a beefsteak dinner (along with all the beer you could drink) on three floors of the DAC with a crowd of over 800 people in the gym for the presentation. That first year, the presence of Jack Dempsey who was an honoree, and Frank Torre (who along with his brother Joe, would become a true friend) added to the dinner. All-Sports Night would run for over 30 years. The list of honorees who have attended this event over the years reads like a Hall-of-Fame roster.

ALL-SPORTS NIGHT

CHAPTER FIVE

ALL-SPORTS NIGHTS HONOREES

BASEBALL

Roy White	Stan Musial	Joe Torre	Willie Mays
Ed Kranepool	Mel Stottlemyre	Tom Seaver	Lou Piniella
Bill Virdon	Dave Kingman	Bob Feller	Phil Rizzuto
Carl Erskine	Ed Lopat	Vic Raschi	Allie Reynolds
Thurman Munson	Duke Snider	Dick Howser	Bill White
Tim McCarver	Rusty Staub	Sal Maglie	Ron Darling
Art Shamsky			

BASKETBALL

Rick Barry	Willis Reed	Dave DeBuscherre	Bob Cousy
Dick Barnett	Arnold "Red" Auerbach	Oscar Robertson	John Havlicek
Frank McGuire	Jamaal Wilkes		

FOOTBALL

Weeb Eubank	Kyle Rote, Sr.	Don Maynard
Irv Cross	Joe Morrison	Earl Campbell

HOCKEY

Rod Gilbert	Phil Esposito	Glen "Chico" Resch

TENNIS Billie Jean King

BOXING Joe Frazier

SOCCER Kyle Rote, Jr.

FITNESS Steve Reeves

SPORTS PERSONALITIES

Mel Allen	Warner Wolf	John W. (Jack) Kaiser	Curt Gowdy

JACK DEMPSEY AT THE FIRST ALL SPORTS NIGHT, WITH COLONEL AL RUSHATZ (L) AND DR. JIM PETERSON (R) OF THE UNITED STATES MILITARY ACADEMY.

COMEDIAN PAT COOPER PERFORMS IN FRONT OF A SOLD-OUT CROWD IN THE
DAC GYM.

The All-Sports Night had credibility because we not only had athletes, but celebrities
as well. We would feature big-time entertainment in the gym, which would be set up like
a theatre. Pat Cooper, the famous comedian, agreed to entertain during one of the
awards nights. He signed on to do ten minutes between the awards ceremonies and
ended up doing thirty-five minutes and left the place rolling in the aisles. He was phe-
nomenal. Tom Gorman, the well-known National League umpire, also used to do comedy for us. He was tremendous, as was Dick Shawn, from *It's a Mad, Mad, Mad, Mad
World.* Dick would perform a skit that had no ending. He would end up falling off stage,
and the lights would come up. The crowd loved it! One of the most popular performers
over the years was Helen O'Connell. She was very beautiful and had the voice to match.
When asked a few years later what some of her career highlights were, O'Connell
responded that among her favorites was performing at the DAC and the way she was
received there. She really put on a terrific show.

After the awards, we would have Dixieland music and a buffet, and the celebrities and
members would end up staying around until two or three o'clock in the morning. Once
the criteria of the award was established and we were able to use the names of the

previous honorees, we never had an athlete turn us down. I never had to pay an athlete to attend either. Granted, we picked up their expenses, but we never had to pay a fee. They enjoyed the tradition of the Club with the Heisman, and it really built upon itself. The DAC became an "in-place" to go for athletes and celebrities. They knew they would be treated well and would enjoy themselves. The stories of some of the great athletes we have honored over the years help illustrate the special "bond" between members of the sports community and the DAC.

SENATOR BILL BRADLEY WITH CARMINE RAGUCCI.

SENATOR BILL BRADLEY

In 1966, I got a call from Marty Glickman, the renowned sports announcer who did the Knick games, asking if he could bring Bill Bradley down to the Club. Bradley wanted a place to work out in the summer. A day or two later, Glickman and Bradley came walking into my office. I'll never forget the skinny Bradley, dressed in khakis and a wrinkled t-shirt; who would've thought that this guy would one day run for President of the United States. Well in those days, the DAC had a dress code that required that all men must wear a tie to come into the lobby. Of course, I didn't make a big deal about it. Bill asked about working out at the Club. I told him the mornings would be best, seeing as how he didn't want to get involved in any games with members. So, he began a ritual of coming in each morning during the summer.

I was fortunate enough to witness a number of his workouts, which were just tremendous. He would concentrate on shooting from certain spots on the floor, and then he would want the ball on the run, shoot off the dribble, and so on. After putting himself through a tiresome shooting workout, he would go to the foul line and shoot 10 foul shots. He always had to make 10 out of 10. Then, off he would go to run a mile in the gym, followed by sit-ups. He would then repeat the whole thing.

Apparently, Bill was off on his shooting because one day he came in on his own with a tape measure and measured the height of the rim in the DAC's gym. A few moments later, he showed up in my office and said to me, "You know, Rudy, your rims are off an inch." So, I had our guys measure them. Sure enough, they were off an inch. And people wonder how he was such a success all those years for the Knicks!

Years later, I hosted a convention for all of the athletic directors and asked Bradley if he would speak. He said sure and did a great job for us, while sharing many stories from his days with the Knicks. A few years after that, around 1987 or 1988, I get a call out of the blue from Senator Bill Bradley. He wanted to know if I would be interested in designing the new Senate gymnasium and fitness center. I told him I didn't know if I was qualified enough or not, but I would be happy to try. A few days later, I get a call from an architect in Washington asking me about my background and inviting me down to Washington. To make a long story short, I got the job to design the new Senate gym and fitness center. Ultimately, with the economy in a little bit of a recession, a public backlash occurred when people found out that the Senate was spending taxpayer dollars on a new gym. The Senate subsequently pulled the money from the project and decided to stay put in the gym they were using. But, I always appreciated that Bill Bradley thought enough of me to recommend that I get the job. He is and always will be a class guy.

THE BROTHERS TORRE

When you look at the individuals honored by the DAC, there are just so many great memories. During my second year at the Club, I met Frank Torre. Frank had retired from baseball, during which time he had a stellar career with the Milwaukee Braves, hitting two home runs against the Yankees to help his team win the '57 World Series. When we met, Frank had just bought into a sporting goods store with which the DAC did business. Frank would supply the trophies for some of the awards nights. In fact, at one of the basketball league award dinners, Frank proposed to his wife Ann. Six children later, he still claims to hold that against me. Frank was always supportive of my work, and introduced me to many major league baseball players. Frank served

JOE TORRE PRESENTS NEW YORK MET ED KRANEPOOL WITH THE DAC "CHAMPIONS AWARD".

as commissioner of the Atlantic Coast Baseball League for a number of years and was instrumental in helping that league grow. Through Frank, I met his brothers—Rocco (a former St. John's player who passed away before he could see his brother Joe's success with the Yankees) and Joe.

Eventually, Joe Torre became a member of the Club and really was very active in DAC activities. He worked out at the Club in the off-season and always attended, and even emceed, many of the Club's events. He was always there to help us out, whether it was a clinic or the kids' Christmas parties. Everyone who knows the Torre brothers are extremely happy for Frank's improving health and Joe's success with the Yankees.

(L-R) MIKE NOONE, FRANK TORRE, GLENN "CHICO" RESCH, TIM MCCARVER, JACK KAISER, JOE TORRE, AND FRANK MCGUIRE AT AN ALL-SPORTS NIGHT DINNER.

Early on, attracting baseball stars like the Torre brothers was significant because most of the stars were available. If they played for the New York teams, we would allow the guys to come in and work out in the off-season at the Club, which was great for our membership. A member might be working out in the weight room, look over, and find himself side-by-side with one of the Yankees or Mets greats.

THREE YANKEE GREATS:
VIC RASCHI, ED LOPAT AND ALLIE REYNOLDS.

RASHI, REYNOLDS, AND LOPAT

As a former Yankee farmhand, a special memory for me occurred when we honored Vic Raschi, Allie Reynolds, and Ed Lopat, the three great Yankee pitchers. Bob Shephard, the renowned Yankee public address announcer, was there that night. As we brought each player up to the stage, Bob would announce him like he was entering the game. "Now pitching for New York, #33, Vic Raschi." Raschi would then come up to the stage where Phil Rizzuto and Mel Allen would reminisce about him. It was a night of nights. It's a shame we didn't videotape that evening because we could all have made a fortune!

I'M NOT SURE THERE IS A CLASSIER GUY THAN CARL ERSKINE. HE HAS ATTENDED A NUMBER OF EVENTS OVER THE YEARS AT THE CLUB.

ALL-SPORTS NIGHT

THURMAN MUNSON

One night, the DAC honored Thurman Munson, and he flew to the event in his own jet. Whenever Thurman would come to the DAC, he would always end up looking at the portraits of the past Heisman winners, commenting on how accurate and well done they were.

I got the idea that we should give Thurman his own portrait, painted by former Philadelphia Eagle player, Tommy McDonald, and his company. Thurman couldn't get over how life-like the picture was. He was very touched. He flew right back after the dinner that evening in his own jet. The whole night became terribly ironic, as later that same year, Thurman was killed in a plane crash. What a tragic loss. He was as great a person as he was a ballplayer.

JOE DIMAGGIO: THE ALL-TIME GREAT

For a three-or four-year period, Joe DiMaggio attended a number of events held at the Club. Joe, in my mind, was a true superstar. The Italians in my neighborhood worshiped Joe D. Joe was a very guarded person and, at times, could be very difficult to deal with. Much has been written about Joe since he passed away. While he was a complex person, no one can debate the fact that he was a true legend in his sport. In all my interactions with Joe, he was always cooperative and respectful to me.

I first saw Joe up close when I was eleven and attended the *New York Journal American Newspaper's* sandlot program at Yankee Stadium. We lived near the newspaper's building on South Street. Rabbit Maranville, the Hall-of-Famer, was director of the sandlot program. He called the neighborhood kids over and gave us tickets for the Saturday clinic and game. We arrived at Yankee Stadium at 9:00 a.m. and were up front for the clinic, which on that day featured Joe DiMaggio and Phil Rizzuto. Following the clinic, a group of kids were allowed on the field for publicity photos that would be featured in the Sunday edition of the newspaper.

My friends were all Italian, and Joe was like a god to them. We were fortunate to be in the group that was allowed on the field. One of my friends, Joe DiSalvo, went up to DiMaggio and put his hands on the number five of Joe's uniform. Joe turned his head to see who was touching him and just smiled. The directors of the program did not find my friend's actions so amusing and had Joe DiSalvo removed from the field. When we got back to our neighborhood, we paraded Joe DiSalvo around, telling anyone who would listen, "These were the hands that touched DiMaggio!" Joe DiSalvo did not wash for a few days until his mother whacked him and made him wash his hands. Needless to say, Joe was upset. None of us has ever forgotten that first encounter with the Yankee Clipper.

My next meeting with Joe DiMaggio took place at the Adirondack Bat Company salute to Willie Mays, put together by Frank Torre, who was a director for Adirondack at the time. Joe was sitting by himself in the back. Eddie Pitcher, who the Club had hired to replace Jim McAtee as the editor of the Club journal, knew Joe and took me over and introduced me. Joe inquired if we were staying for the dinner, and then invited us to sit with him. I was both surprised and excited. We joined Joe for dinner—an event that is still very vivid in my mind. I can recall every little detail about that night.

Joe's first visit to the DAC took place at a Salute to Boxing Greats dinner, as a guest of "Big" Julie Weintraub, the Las Vegas sports entrepreneur. Joe, always concerned about his privacy, was

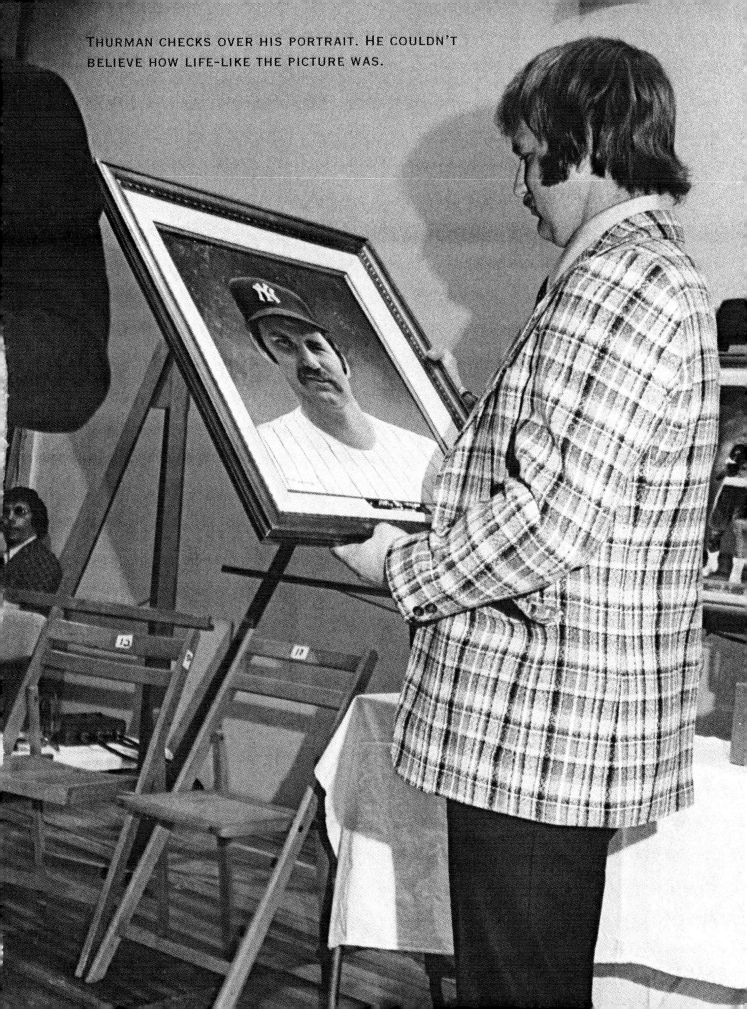

THURMAN CHECKS OVER HIS PORTRAIT. HE COULDN'T
BELIEVE HOW LIFE-LIKE THE PICTURE WAS.

a bit apprehensive about attending, and at the private reception before the dinner, he chastised some of the members for abusing requests for photos and autographs. I asked Julie if Joe would like to present one of the awards in the ring. Julie responded that this would not be a good idea with Joe being uptight that night. During dinner, Joe began to relax and at the fights (Joe was a great boxing fan), he really began to enjoy himself. Before we knew what was happening, Joe came into the ring to present some awards.

When Sal Schirillo of *Street and Smith's* Sports Group asked me if I would run their 50th Anniversary Baseball Magazine dinner at the Club, I contacted Joe about attending and receiving the lifetime achievement award. Joe asked who would be the beneficiaries of the evening, and I told him the proceeds were to go to the Baseball Assistance Team. Joe accepted. Stan "The Man" Musial was present. Bob Feller was there. Willie McCovey was in attendance. Bob Gibson was there. It was a star-studded cast to say the least.

I was to send a limousine to pick up Joe at the airport. Well, however it happened, the limo screwed up and never showed. By the time Joe got to the DAC, he was really ticked off. I went up to his room, and he let me have it. Fortunately, I brought along some gifts (a couple of new golf shirts, a couple of sleeves of golf balls, things I knew he would like). Joe always seemed to back off a little bit if you were smart enough to bring him a gift!

During the reception that night, I made a big mistake in not providing for extra security for all the baseball greats in attendance. The autograph collectors were out in full force, particularly zeroing in on Joe, who was furious and threatened not to participate in the awards program. It was about this time that the memorabilia shops were sprouting up all over the place, and guys were selling autographed items for some pretty good money. I had my brother Steve and his friends surround Joe to provide him with some relief from the autograph hounds. During the awards program, we also provided extra security for Joe, so that when he was announced as the greatest living player, he came up to the podium and surprised me by speaking for fifteen minutes, electrifying the audience.

After the dinner, we showed the Buster Douglas/Evander Holyfield fight on closed circuit television in a private area. Joe asked me to sit with him and thanked me for a great night. Go figure that out! The next day, I had to attend a meeting out of the building, and when I arrived at the Club later that afternoon, the front desk said Joe was looking for me. I thought Joe had checked out already. I tracked him down in the third-floor steam room. Joe was in a great mood, and as we sat together over a drink, he asked me if I would like to go to a theatre in Greenwich Village to see the movie *GoodFellas*. The movie was about the mob and wiseguys and all of that. Joe didn't like the movie because of all the profanity in it. I could hear Joe cussing under his breath at some guy a couple of rows ahead of us, who had brought his two young boys with him. Joe didn't think that young boys should be watching such a profanity-laced movie and let the guy know about it. Again, that was just the kind of guy Joe was.

Back at the Club, I thanked Joe and told him that a car was all set to take him to the airport the next morning. I had forgotten to have the special poster that Street and Smith's had made for the 50th Anniversary dinner signed, so I told the front desk receptionist to please ask Joe to sign it before he left. When I came in the next day, she told me that when she asked Joe to sign the posters, he threw them on the floor and stormed out to

AN AMERICAN ICON AND ONE OF MY HEROES, JOE DiMAGGIO SIGNS AN AUTOGRAPH AFTER ONE OF OUR FIGHT NIGHTS AS JOE PONTE AND I LOOK ON.

D.A.C. Salutes BOXING GREATS

NEW YORK CITY
NOVEMBER 21 1978

his car. Five minutes later, he returned and said, "Were these for Rudy?" When she replied "yes," he signed them.

Even though he had a pacemaker, Joe loved the steamroom at the DAC. One time, we were getting ready to take a steam, and Joe had about $4,000 in his pocket. He turned and asked what he should do with all this money. I told him to give it to me to lock up in my office. So, I give Joe an envelope, and he puts the money in it, licks it, and seals it. He then grabs a pen and starts making these little lines across the back of the envelope. I asked Joe, "What the hell are you doing?" And he turned plain as day, and said, "Just in case they try to open and steal it!" And I said, "But you're giving it to me, Joe!!"

To this day I have an autographed picture in my office of Joe and Mickey Mantle. When I had Mickey sign the picture, I asked him if he remembered that picture and he looked at it and asked what I meant. I told him that it was taken on the occasion of the first Yankees Old-Timers Day that he came back for and that they introduced him last, breaking protocol which was to announce the oldest living Yankee legend last. They decided to make Mantle last because he was so popular in the minds of younger fans. The fans applauded him for almost ten minutes. Joe was very angry that he had to stand out there waiting, and you could tell he was upset during the National Anthem. When Joe finally made it into the dugout, he commented to Bob Fisher, the Yankees public relations guy at the time, that this would be his last time attending. As a result, Joe didn't come back until Steinbrenner brought him back years later. That was just the kind of guy he was.

For a number of years, the Club hosted the Golden Spikes award that is presented annually to the outstanding collegiate baseball player. The year that Robin Ventura won the award, we had Joe DiMaggio as the guest of honor. Recently, Robin gave an interview where he said that receiving the award from Joe was the biggest moment of his life. At that luncheon, Ann Ligouri (who has become a television personality) was just starting

ROBIN VENTURA AT THE GOLDEN SPIKES AWARD LUNCHEON. ROBIN HAS SAID RECEIVING THE AWARD FROM JOE DIMAGGIO WAS THE BIGGEST MOMENT OF HIS LIFE.

out in radio, and asked me if I could arrange for her to interview Joe. I asked Joe about the request, and he said it was okay. I told Ann not to ask any questions about Marilyn Monroe or other topics that might be too personal for Joe. I went back to my office, and after a while, Joe walked in and proceeded to bawl me out. I was a bit dumbstruck and wondered what had happened. I stayed up that next night to listen to the interview on the radio and thought that Ann was great. The next time I saw Joe, I made it a point to ask him why he became so angry. His answer was, "I wasn't angry. The luncheon was great!"

One of the most memorable occasions with Joe was when I was down in Florida, and Joe was to cut the ribbon on a housing complex built with a sports and fitness theme. Prior to the evening's festivities, a luncheon for the mayor of Miami and other dignitaries was held at the Fountain Bleu Hotel. Following the lunch, Joe invited my brother and I to sit with him in a private area, and for the next three hours, we talked baseball. If I only could have taped that conversation. Joe gave us inside knowledge about the great players of his time and much of his philosophy. I will miss Joe, but the photos and my memories of the times with him will last forever.

LEFTY GOMEZ AND MICKEY MANTLE AT A DAC RECEPTION.

BOBBY THOMSON BLUE PLATE SPECIAL

Bobby Thomson has always been great to the Club, consistently coming back for the New York Giants reunions we've held. One of the times he was here, he told me an interesting story about the "shot heard round the world." The Giants were in a three-game play-off with Brooklyn. The first game was at Ebbetts Field, and Bobby played great, hitting a home run that was very instrumental in their winning. In the second game, which was at the Polo Grounds, he was terrible. Bobby struck out with the bases loaded and made a costly error in the field. Bobby was a quiet man, always has been and still is. At the time, he was single and living with his mother in Staten Island. A group of friends from Staten Island, Dominic Coppatelli among them, were waiting for Bobby after the game to take him home. Bobby was so upset over his performance that he didn't want to go home right away because he knew he would only end up taking it out on his mother. Dominic Coppatelli was a member of the DAC and suggested heading over to the Club for dinner. To this day, Bobby can't remember what he ate, but he said he just relaxed so much, all of the tension left him. The next day, he went out and hit his famous home run. Years later, I told him it was too bad he couldn't remember what he ate that night because we would serve it every year on that particular date and call it the "Bobby Thomson Special!"

BOBBY THOMSON AND FAMILY ON THE EVENING WE HONORED BOBBY AND "THE SHOT HEARD ROUND THE WORLD".

Another great night occurred when we had Oscar Robertson at the DAC. The Big O came in a day early and decided to get a workout in. About 11:30 in the morning, he headed up to the gymnasium for a run with a towel around his neck and a sweat suit on. As he was running in the gym, the lunch-time basketball players were beginning to convene. Short one guy, someone yelled out to Oscar to play, not recognizing who he was. Oscar said he would rather just run, but further persistence by this heavyset loudmouth got Oscar to toss off his towel and head for the court. The loudmouth player told his team …"he'll guard the black guy." First time down the floor, Oscar got the ball, put a dazzling move on the overmatched defender, and scored. This scene was repeated several times over the course of the entire game.

The next night during the awards dinner, Oscar got up to deliver his speech. As he looked out into the crowd he recognized the gentleman whom he had embarrassed on the court the day before. It finally dawned on the guy who his opponent was. Of course, Oscar wouldn't let him off the hook too easily and with a smile shouted, "I don't think you can guard this black guy!"

MIKE NOONE WITH CURT GOWDY AND OSCAR ROBERTSON, WHO SHOW OFF THEIR CHAMPIONS AWARDS.

BOB HOPE, ON A BREAK FROM
SHOOTING THE FINAL SCENE
OF "THE PRIVATE NAVY OF
SERGEANT O'FARRELL,"
TAKES TIME FOR A PHOTO OP.

As the scope and number of day-to-day Club athletic activities expanded and the special sport programs became annual events that everyone looked forward to, some very special moments occurred at the Club.

HOLLYWOOD
AT THE DAC

We were fortunate enough over the years to have a couple of movies shoot scenes at the DAC. One of those movies, *The Private Navy of Sergeant O'Farrell*, featured the great Bob Hope and Phyllis Diller. The directors decided to re-shoot one of the final scenes of the film, which was supposed to take place in the middle of water. Unfortunately, it was the month of December, not the most conducive time to be shooting in water in the Big Apple. When it became known that Diller, who was going to be in New York City to do a couple of shows, and Hope, who was in New York City preparing to head overseas to entertain the troops, were both available to shoot the last scene again, the directors quickly scoured the city for a place that had a pool. At the time, the DAC was one of the few clubs in the city that did. The directors asked permission to use the DAC pool to shoot the last scene and, of course, we said yes. It was quite an honor to have Bob Hope and Phyllis Diller in the Club. At that particular time, Bob and Phyllis were among the biggest stars in the entertainment industry.

PHYLLIS WANTED TO SEE THE HEISMAN TROPHY. SHE WAS SOMETHING ELSE—SHE HAD US LAUGHING THE WHOLE TIME.

RYAN O'NEAL DURING SHOOTING OF LOVE STORY. NOTE THE CUT ABOVE HIS EYE.

The scene called for Phyllis Diller to pop out of the water and surprise Hope. I remember the set directors had to build a table and rig it up underwater for Phyllis because she couldn't swim. It was quite a production, but they finally got the scene completed after about four hours of filming. If you ever see that movie, those last few scenes where it looks like they are in the ocean were actually filmed in the DAC pool.

I invited Bob Hope to dinner in the Club restaurant that evening, thinking this would be a great opportunity to show the president of the DAC, John Ott, what a great impact bringing sports stars and celebrities into the Club could have on members and membership enrollment. I believe my point came across loud and clear that evening.

This led to many more involvements with Bob Hope. He would tape his annual Christmas show in New York right before the Heisman dinner, which allowed him to highlight both the Associated Press All-American team and the Heisman Trophy winner. Bob would always make sure we were invited to his show, which gave us the chance to greet our Heisman winner prior to the Heisman dinner and activities later that week.

The same company that arranged for the Bob Hope filming in the pool called to see if they could shoot in our squash court and executive locker room for the movie *Love Story* starring Ryan O'Neal. We agreed to allow them to shoot as long as it didn't conflict with the member's usage of the facilities.

Prior to the shoot in the squash courts, I offered to have our squash instructor show Ryan some of the different moves of the game to make it more genuine, but Ryan assured me that he was an avowed squash aficionado. They weren't ten minutes into shooting the scene when O'Neal got out of position and received a blow to the head that required stitches and delayed shooting for a couple of days!

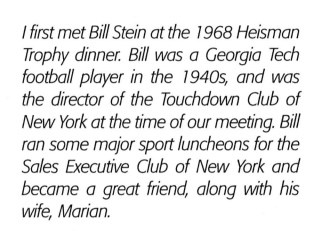

I first met Bill Stein at the 1968 Heisman Trophy dinner. Bill was a Georgia Tech football player in the 1940s, and was the director of the Touchdown Club of New York at the time of our meeting. Bill ran some major sport luncheons for the Sales Executive Club of New York and became a great friend, along with his wife, Marian.

FOOTBALL
ROUNDUP
EXEMPLARY PLAYER
AWARDS DINNER

CHAPTER SEVEN

Bill introduced me to Adrian Lopez, who was the publisher of the *Football Roundup Magazine*, one of about 20 different magazines he published. Adrian and his editor Herb Furlow came up with the idea to create a football dinner, and we gave it the name "The *Football Roundup Magazine's* Exemplary Player of the Year Awards." The idea was to honor both a major college player and a small college (Division II or III) player each year.

In order to get the award supported by Club members, I turned to my friends in the handball club. They were really a bunch of great guys who were very receptive to some of the new ideas that I had brought to the Club. They made sure tickets were sold for the awards dinner. Of course, once we did the first dinner, it was pretty easy to sell-out since the occasion featured a virtual who's who in the football world in attendance. Over the years we've had Joe Thiesmann, Ed "Too Tall" Jones, Walter Payton, Randy White, Ricky Bell, Hugh Green, and Jim Plunkett, just to name a few. In 1975, we added the All-Pro Awards, honoring past professional football greats such as Alan Ameche, Gayle Sayers, Y.A. Tittle, Paul Hornung and Jim Taylor of the Green Bay Packers… a pretty elite group of individuals.

PAUL HORNUNG, ADRIAN LOPEZ, HERB FURLOW, AND JIM TAYLOR. WITHOUT ADRIAN AND HERB, WE NEVER WOULD HAVE BEEN ABLE TO HOLD THE DINNERS TO HONOR EXCEPTIONAL ATHLETES LIKE HORNUNG AND TAYLOR.

These were very successful evenings for the Club and allowed our membership to mix and mingle with some of the biggest names in sports. When *Football Roundup Magazine* went out of business, we began a close relationship with *Street & Smith's Magazine*. It really is a shame that video cameras weren't more prevalent during this time. When the celebrities and athletes went back to the third Floor or Heisman Room, you really got a chance to see them in a relaxed state. They were among their own. Many times, they were among teammates or friends they hadn't seen in years, all of which made for some great reminiscing.

THE GREAT GALE SAYERS.

FORMER GRAMBLING COACH EDDIE ROBINSON. IT IS AMAZING TO THINK OF THE NUMBER OF YOUNG MEN HE HAS IMPACTED OVER HIS REMARKABLE COACHING CAREER.

"HE WAS AND STILL IS A NATURAL-BORN EVENT PLANNER"

— SAL SCHILIRO

STREET & SMITH'S SPORTS GROUP

"I first met Rudy in 1980, during the time I was publisher of *Sport* magazine. We developed a friendship that has endured for more than twenty years. I recognized immediately that Rudy had a knack for putting people together. He could bring people to the table from a variety of areas to achieve a positive end result. He was and still is a natural-born event planner.

(L-R) KERRY KITTLES, DAVE BING, RICK PITINO, AND SAL SCHILIRO

"It wasn't long before Rudy began presenting event ideas to me, usually dinners that would be held at the Downtown Athletic Club. Rudy's suggestion was that *Street and Smith's* would sponsor a series of baseball, football and basketball dinners where we would honor players and coaches from the professional and collegiate ranks. *Street and Smith's* would honor the player of the year, coach of the year, and a legend of the game at a gala banquet held at the DAC. Always a sell-out crowd, the excitement and electricity generated at these events were incredible!

(L-R) P.J. CARLIESIMO, SEAN ELLIOT, SAL SCHILIRO, LUTE OLSON AND BOB KNIGHT.

"Over the years, the *Street and Smith's* events involved many fun-filled evenings, honoring sport greats like Jim Brown, Stan Musial, Bill Parcels, Rick Pitino and Bob Knight, just to name a few. The 1990 baseball dinner stands out as the most exciting of all. *Street and Smith's* was celebrating the 50th anniversary of its baseball edition, and the magazine conducted a yearlong poll among past and present players, coaches, and sportswriters to name the best players over that fifty-year period. These players were then invited to a dinner held in their honor at the DAC. Normally, a capacity crowd at the DAC is 300 people in any one of the main dining rooms. The demand was so great for this event, however, that we divided the crowd into two dining rooms of 300 people each with no dais, and then we had everyone move to the gymnasium for the presentations. More than 600 people filled the DAC gym to hear the co-emcees, Rusty Staub and Fran Healy (the duo were the broadcast team of the Mets at the time) make the presentations.

"The list of honorees that evening was truly a who's who of baseball. Baseball luminaries like Joe DiMaggio, Bob Feller, Bob Gibson, Willie McCovey, Yogi Berra, Stan Musial, Bobby Doerr, Ozzie Smith, Gary Carter and Keith Hernandez were just some of the baseball stars who were in attendance.

"The building was rocking with excitement. I remember sitting at dinner with Joe DiMaggio, who was not in a particularly good mood at that point. He kept asking about the proceeds for the dinner and who was profiting from the event. I assured him that all of the proceeds were going to the Baseball Assistance Team, but I'm not sure that he was convinced. He was being hounded for autographs, which he would not sign. Joe also told me more than once that I should not expect him to speak, so I need not bother to call him to the dais.

"Well, by the end of the evening, DiMaggio had done a complete turn-around. Rusty and Fran announced each player, each player's accomplishments were read and then he was asked to come to the podium. Each player received a rousing ovation from the crowd. I cannot begin to describe the crowd reaction to the introduction of DiMaggio. It was the loudest and longest standing ovation I had ever witnessed, and he was visibly moved. So much so, that DiMaggio arose, and slowly walked to the podium to speak. For a guy who was so adamant about not wanting to speak, we had a tough time getting him to stop! He reminisced about the old Yankee teams and the many championships they had won. He also spoke about Casey Stengel, Ted Williams and much, much more. Then, to the delight of the crowd, he actually invited people to come forward and said he would gladly sign autographs. It was, to say the least, a very special night for not only me, but for everyone in attendance—an evening that we will never forget.

"An event like this *was* the DAC. This event *was* Rudy Riska. Only Rudy could have put a night like this together."

—Sal Schiliro

"TOO TALL" JONES

Ed "Too Tall" Jones really made quite an impression on everyone with whom he came in contact during his stay at the DAC. Too Tall came from a background that didn't afford him very nice (or warm) clothes, and he had very little money when he showed up at the DAC for the awards dinner. Fortunately for Too Tall, a representative for the Dallas Cowboys, I believe it was Gil Brandt, was on hand at the Club and took Too Tall out and got him a new leather coat, as well as sticking a little spending money in his pocket. That was all Too Tall needed to have the time of his life in New York City. After returning from a night out on the

EVEN MAYOR GIULIANI TOOK THE OPPORTUNITY TO ATTEND RUDY'S EVENTS!

town, Too Tall decided to keep the party going up in his room at the DAC. Apparently, old Too Tall had the music and dancing going a little too loud for one of our other guests who was staying in the room one floor below. So, this guy thought he would go up and give whoever was making all this racket, which was Too Tall of course, a piece of his mind. Storming up the stairs he went. He got to the room where the music was blaring and pounded on the door, ready to lay into whoever answered. The door swung open and there was Too Tall, all 6'6" and 275 pounds of him. The little guy who pounded on the door was looking straight up, with his mouth hanging open. Too Tall figures the way that guy ran away from his room, he could have suited up and played wide-out for the Cowboys! I don't know if we've ever had any player come in who has enjoyed his stay at the DAC quite like Ed "Too Tall" Jones.

(L-R) IRV CROSS, JACK WHITAKER, ED "TOO TALL" JONES, RANDY GRADISHAR, AND CARMINE RAGUCCI.

SWEETNESS

Walter Payton was another great player who really turned heads when he showed up for the awards dinner. You have to remember Walter was a little-known player out of Jackson State. Nobody knew at that time he would go on to become the NFL's all-time leading rusher. Walter decided to get a workout in while he was at the Club. After lifting some weights, he decided to shoot around in the gymnasium. In a matter of minutes, the 5'9" Payton was dunking the basketball every way imaginable to the utter disbelief of those DAC members in the gym that day. His explosiveness and leg power were absolutely awesome. If I was smart, I would have realized right there, I was watching a sure-fire Hall-of-Famer and asked to be his agent! Oh well.

(L-R) ADRIAN LOPEZ, RANDY WHITE, WALTER PAYTON, AND IRV CROSS. BOTH RANDY AND WALTER HAD JUST RECENTLY ENTERED THE NATIONAL FOOTBALL LEAGUE.

A KID IN A CANDY STORE

I remember the year we invited Neil Lomax from Portland State. The folks at Portland State couldn't believe that Neil was getting invited to the Downtown Athletic Club—home of the Heisman. To top it off, Lomax, already a quiet kid, was in awe of Jim Plunkett, who was being honored at the same dinner as the Super Bowl MVP. The day after the dinner, I was planning to take Plunkett up to Yankee Stadium to meet some of the Yankees. So, I invited Neil to stay a couple of extra days at the Club and tag along with Plunkett and me. Neil was like a kid in a candy store. He seemed to really appreciate the fact that we kept him around the few extra days, instead of just giving him an award and sending him on his way.

WHERE ARE THE FRANKFURTERS?

One of the great stories from the Football Awards Dinners occurred the year we honored a number of the great Baltimore Colts players. There was a tremendous snowstorm that day, but they all showed up. The tradition for these dinners was to serve the meal on three designated floors, followed by entertainment in the gymnasium which would be set up theater-style. After the entertainment, we would serve a buffet, which usually consisted of hot dogs and beer on the 3rd Floor. Well, I came walking into the 3rd Floor, and right away observed the legendary Art Donovan sitting at a table over in the corner with a Styrofoam cooler. It seems Art drank only Schlitz beer. So, instead of taking a chance that the beverage of his choice wouldn't be served that evening, he brought along his own

(L-R) DICK LYNCH, CARMINE RAGUCCI, HUGH GREEN OF PITT, JIM PLUNKETT (WHO HAD JUST WON SUPER BOWL MVP HONORS), NFL HALL OF FAMER TOMMY McDONALD, AND NEIL LOMAX OF PORTLAND STATE.

supply. Just before the night was over, it must have been about midnight, I see a waiter bring over a big tray of hot dogs and Art slipped him a $20. I asked Art what he was doing, and Art said, "I'm heading up to my room now to eat."

About eight or nine years later, we were honoring Don Shula, the legendary head coach of the Miami Dolphins, who had also coached the Baltimore Colts earlier in his career. Of course, Art was present that evening, but the program had changed a little bit from his earlier visit. We now served dinner on the 15th Floor of the DAC for everyone, had the entertainment in the gym, and then headed to the Heisman Room for a night-cap. All night long, Art kept looking over at me, almost glaring at me. For the life of me, I couldn't figure out what the problem was. I did know, however, that Art Donovan was not a guy you wanted glaring at you, so I went over and asked him what the problem was. Art asked, "Where's the frankfurters?" Apparently, that was all this guy ever ate—salami, bologna and frankfurters. Seeing how upset he was, I decided I better do something, so I grabbed one of the limousine drivers and asked him to run up to Katz's Delicatessen on Houston Street and bring back some bologna, salami and stuff for Art. When the driver returned, Art was so happy I think I saw a tear of joy roll down his face. He certainly was one of the classic individuals at the Football Awards dinners.

A COLT'S REUNION: (L-R) ALAN AMECHE, ART DONOVAN, RAY BERRY AND GINO MARCHETTI.

JERRY COONEY RAISES THE HAND OF CURRENT
"CZAR" OF BOXING AT THE DAC JOHN TURCO.

Jim McAtee, the editor of the Club's journal and a friend who supported my work, was leaving the Club, forcing us to look for a replacement. I first met Eddie Pitcher at Yankee Stadium when we would visit with Jerry Coleman (commissioner of the Atlantic Coast Baseball League) in the pressroom. Eddie worked for the player agent Frank Scott. Frank was closing out his business, and Eddie called me at just the right time. So, I set up an interview for him with the DAC's publications committee. They hired Eddie, who proceeded to do a really great job, using the magazine to promote and market the Club. He was especially helpful in promoting the series of sport dinners and events I organized. Eddie had a boxing background. One day, he brought a gentleman to the club who had just written a book with the great boxing champion, Willie Pep, called "Friday's Heroes," about the great Friday night fights from Madison Square Garden that Gillette Blue Blades used to sponsor on the radio.

SALUTE TO BOXING GREATS

CHAPTER EIGHT

(L-R) Joe Ponte—Chair of Boxing at the DAC, Joey Maxim—former light heavyweight champ, Joe Frazier, and the great trainer Eddie Futch.

My father always listened to sports on the radio (we were both baseball fans of the New York Giants, which was tough living in a neighborhood of Yankee/DiMaggio rooters). He particularly enjoyed listening to Don Dunphy (who later became a good friend of mine) and Bill Corum create the images of the great pugilistic warriors who fought on Friday evenings in front of a packed house at the Garden. Suffice it to say, I was a big boxing fan and loved the book on Pep that brought back all my boyhood memories.

Friday's Heroes was written by Bob Sacchi. Bob was not only a boxing buff, but a Humphrey Bogart lookalike, and he created a whole act around that. We decided to throw a dinner to help promote the book and chose to honor Jersey Joe Walcott. Because the dinner was held right before Thanksgiving, we gave everyone in attendance a turkey that they could take home for Thanksgiving. Bob Sacchi dressed up like Bogart and sang "My Way" to Joe Walcott, who broke down and cried. What a night!

The DAC has had a long history with the sport of boxing, even going so far as to stage boxing matches during the war years to help raise money for cigarettes for the American GIs. In my early days at the club, I ran the annual Boys Club of New York fundraising boxing nights, which were supported by the Wall Street groups and generated substantial monies for the Boys Club. Marty Bunce, who became the director of the Boys Club and a great friend, worked tirelessly with me on making this a successful annual event.

PAST DAC PRESIDENT JACK FARRELL HELPS WELCOME BILLY CONN TO THE CLUB.

Don Scanlon, Jr., who was a DAC member and in attendance the night that we honored Jersey Joe, was involved in collegiate boxing at Villanova and asked if he could put on a fight at the DAC. Of course I said "yes." Unfortunately, it wasn't that successful.

What that night did do, however, was give me the idea of combining the two events. We called the night "Salute to Boxing Greats" and honored some of the all-time great professional fighters while also having a card of collegiate boxing matches. To spice things up even more, we got permission from the Rocky Marciano family to create the Rocky Marciano Award, which would be awarded to "a champion in life and a champion in the ring." The first Salute to Boxing Greats was again held just prior to Thanksgiving. Similar to festivities involving Jersey Joe Walcott, we again passed out turkeys to every single person in attendance. These nights ran for 20 years, and we truly had the greats of boxing show up. To this day, most people find it hard to believe who we got to honor at these events... Tony Zale, who had the great fights with Rocky Graziano, Billy Conn, Floyd Patterson, and Archie Moore, just to name a few—a virtual who's who of the boxing world.

JACK AND DIANE DEMPSEY WITH JOE PONTE.

Alex Arguello showed up for a Salute to Boxing Greats night, just two weeks after taking a beating from Aaron Pryor. In fact, at one time or another, Muhammad Ali, George Foreman, and Joe Frazier all came to watch the fights.

It was a dream come true for the college fighters who would attend the afternoon press conference featuring the big name pro fighters and get a chance to get autographs and mingle with their heroes. To this day, I often bump into someone who fought at the DAC when he was in college, and every last one of them says it was the greatest night of their lives. Not only did the college kids get the thrill of fighting in front of a crowd of 1,000 people, many of whom were sportwriters and celebrities, but we honored many of their heroes as well. It's too bad that the Boxing Night is no longer held at the DAC. Unfortunately, the club changed from a social club to more of a workout club for the Wall Street crowd. Back in the 50s, 60s, and 70s, the guys were able to relate to the athletes and really respected them and enjoyed having them at the Club.

THREE OF THE GREAT HEAVYWEIGHT FIGHTERS OF ALL TIME: ARCHIE MOORE, GEORGE FOREMAN AND JOE FRAZIER ATTENDING A FIGHT NIGHT AT THE CLUB.

THE GREATEST!

The night that the great Muhammad Ali was honored, he and Joe Frazier ended up in the ring together. Joking around, both started to take their sportcoats off like they were gonna go at it! Then, they both turned to the reporters and stated, "We're crazy for fighting for free!" They were right. Ali signed 900 autographs that night. What a class act, a really genuine guy.

Seeing Joe Frazier with Ali in the ring and Arthur Mercante Sr. at ringside, it brought back memories of the first fight between them on March 8, 1971 that Mercante refereed. I received a phone call the day before this historic fight from the Detectives Association inviting me to be their guest. I readily accepted and agreed to meet them at a sports bar across from Madison Square Garden. When we left the bar to head over to the Garden, the guys I was with from the Detectives Association said they had to get some things out of their car. What they got was a black bag with armbands for us to wear that had "Bomb Squad" printed on them.

As we approached the various checkpoints around the Garden, we were waved on. Once inside the Garden, one of the detectives had us take off the armbands and put them back in the bag. He then discarded the bag. I was told I was on my own with regards to where to watch the fight. So much for thinking that I was being treated as a special guest! Not knowing where to go, I subsequently bumped into John Condon, the head of boxing at the Garden. I told John the story of my invite. He laughed and gave me a special button to wear that would allow me to stand anywhere in the Garden. The night becomes more special to me as the years go by. I can always claim that for a brief time, I was a member of the NYPD Bomb Squad!

Every time Ali stayed at the DAC, he was always willing to help us out. On numerous occasions over the years, we worried about the possibility of big-time celebrities who have a big entourage, which Ali had, leaving town and sticking the DAC with the bill. Ali never did that. In fact, he always made sure that he let us know exactly who was with him, because there were always hangers-on trying to pass themselves off as part of Ali's entourage. Far too often, Ali was just too nice a guy to chase them off.

Beekman Hospital, a famous hospital in downtown Manhattan, was sponsoring a health fair at the World Trade Center during one of the times that Ali was staying at the DAC. They had offered me a booth at the trade show at the fair to show off the Heisman Trophy and publicize the Club as a favor for some of the things I had done for their sports medicine department. So, of course, I got to thinking about having Ali come by the booth for a little while. I spoke to Muhammad about it, and he said sure and asked if he could sell autographed copies of the Koran while he was sitting at the booth. I said I would ask the hospital people. So, I called them up and asked if they would like to have Muhammad Ali make an appearance at the show. Of course they said sure, and in lieu of any type of appearance fee, they said that they had no problem with Ali selling his autographed books. Ali and I got to the trade show about 11:30 am and there was a small line outside where people would go through all of the different free tests—blood pressure, vision, etc. Well, the rumor got out that Ali was at the trade show, and the next thing we know, the Port Authority had to call out the police because the line was around the building. Everyone wanted to get in and see Muhammad Ali, who of course, sold out of all his books!

In the early 60s, the need to be physically fit started to become a big deal in the American mindset. In the process, I got to become pretty good friends with a gentleman by the name of Bob Stewart, who was Stan Musial's assistant. Bob had been the athletic director at St. Louis University, as well as a great basketball player at Syracuse University. Bob was the guy who coined the term, "President's Council on Physical Fitness" and subsequently added "Sports" to it. The Council started doing a lot of promotions and tie-ins with the NFL. Stan Musial was the chairman of the Council, which is how Bob got tied in with it.

PRESIDENT'S COUNCIL ON PHYSICAL FITNESS

CHAPTER NINE

At the time, the popularity of a number of fitness-related activities, such as aerobics, jogging and strength training, was sky-rocketing at the Club as well. As a result, the Club leaders saw fit to convert a dining room floor into a fitness center to accommodate the increased interest in fitness. Exercise equipment was added to the center slowly at first, but with help from our good friends at West Point, Dr. Jim Peterson and Colonel Al Rushatz, along with Club member Aubrey Seaman, we soon had a fitness center second-to-none. We hired a fitness director, Paul Mastropasqua (Mr. New Jersey), who later became the fitness director for the Mets, Braves and Yankees. Dr. Harold Hermann served

OLYMPIAN MARYLOU RETTON SQUEEZES IN BETWEEN JULIUS "DR.J" ERVING AND JAMAAL WILKES.

BILL STEIN, BUSTER CRABBE, AND STEVE REEVES. WE WERE FORTUNATE TO HAVE STEVE GIVE US PERMISSION TO USE HIS NAME IN ASSOCIATION WITH OUR FITNESS AWARD.

on a variety of committees at the Club and helped develop the DAC's sports medical committee, along with John Mandel and Dr. Irwin Sharkey.

With the explosion in the interest in physical fitness taking off, I decided to create a number of new programs, like the 500-Mile Jogging Club and the 500-Mile Swimming Club. Out of all of this, the President's Council on Physical Fitness Awards Dinner was born. The dinner would be an opportunity to honor the top athletes at the club who took part in the many competitive programs run throughout the year, as well as invite in some big-name celebrities and legends of fitness. I had been lucky enough to meet Steve Reeves, who had played Hercules in the movies and was internationally renowned as one of the all-time great bodybuilders. Steve had an extraordinary physique. I asked Steve if the DAC could name an award after him that honored athletes that used weight training and fitness to strengthen their careers. Thus, the Steve Reeves Award was created. Coupled with the President's Council on Physical Fitness Award, we were able to attract some big-name people to the DAC's fitness awards dinner. Over the years, individuals, like Buster Crabb, Jack LaLane, Rocky Bleier, Al Oerter, Rafer Johnson, Julius Erving, MaryLou Retton and the great Don Imus, participated in this event.

OVER THE YEARS, THE DAC HAS HONORED A NUMBER OF INDIVIDUALS FOR THEIR EFFORTS INVOLVING PHYSICAL FITNESS, INCLUDING DAN LURIE, DONNA DEVARONA, ROCKEY BLIER, AND JIM JENSEN—SHOWN WITH STEVE REEVES (SECOND FROM THE LEFT).

Don Imus has truly become an icon in New York City. His morning radio show (also shown nationally on cable television) draws a diverse audience that ranges from the top politicians, media and print personalities to the average guy or gal making a living. Behind the microphone and at the radio studio, there is no one better than Imus.

Some may see Imus' name tied in with a physical fitness award and wonder what this world has come to. Let me explain. My daughter used to listen to Imus in the morning back in the days when he regularly played music on his show. During that period, I always tried to get up and have breakfast with my kids before we all went our separate ways. One particular morning, my daughter had Imus on, and he said to his sidekick, Charles McCord, that they had been invited to the Fight Night at the DAC. I knew nothing of this, so when I came into the Club I immediately tried to find out who had invited this guy. Apparently, the controller of the Club at that time had given a couple of tickets to the guy who made sure our elevators and alarm system were working right. I told our controller that there were no tickets to be had; we were all sold out. Of course, he told me that he had to have tickets because the elevator repairman was bringing this guy—Don Imus—with him. So, I called the elevator repairman in and told him I would get him four tickets if Imus promised to bring Mike Lupica along with him. A couple of years earlier Lupica, the noted sports journalist, had come down on the Heisman and the Club, saying it was a place for old drunks. I wanted Lupica to see how many young people worked out at the Club. Of course, he was entitled to his opinion, but if he was going to share his opinion I felt he should at least have his facts straight.

Lupica and Imus showed up early for the reception hour. I had my buddy Dick Lynch, the long-time football Giants announcer, give Lupica a tour of the facilities. After the tour, Lupica came up and apologized for what he had written a couple of years earlier, telling me it was based on just a couple of guys he had met and that he shouldn't have made a rash generalization about the entire Club. Imus, meanwhile, wanted to watch the closed-circuit championship fight between Gerry Cooney and Larry Holmes. I noticed Imus kept looking at me. I was sitting next to Charles McCord, and Charles and I were getting along pretty good. Turns out he was from Springfield, Missouri, and we had some mutual friends. Other than "hello" and "goodbye", I didn't say much to Imus all night.

The next morning, I sat down for breakfast to hear what Imus has to say about the Club. He gave us a few ribs, but for the most part, he provided the DAC with a good plug. I didn't think too much about it. That Sunday morning, my daughter and I decided to go for a run. Out where I live in Bayridge, Brooklyn, there is a place called Show Road Park that runs along the water. It is a five-mile stretch that people bike and jog along. My daughter and I were out there jogging, and all of a sudden, I saw this guy running towards us. I couldn't believe it, but it was none other than Don Imus. I had a hat on so he didn't recognize me, but as he passed, I yelled, "Imus", which startled him. He came over, and I introduced my daughter to him and that was it.

The following Monday morning, I was listening to his show, and he was telling Charles McCord about meeting me, only he couldn't remember my name, so he calls me Zippy on the air. "I met Zippy out jogging Sunday," he said. Over the next couple of months, we bumped into each other out on Show Park Road a few times.

New York City radio and television personality Don Imus—a recipient of the DAC's Fitness Award—with his sidekick, Charles McCord.

Some time later, we scheduled a Comedy Night at the DAC, and it was going to be a flop, unless we sold some more tickets. I was asked if I could get Imus to talk about it on his show. So, I called his producer at the time, a guy by the name of Mark Schiff, and asked if Imus could give us a plug. Schiff surprised me, and asked if we wouldn't mind doing a little roast of Don Imus at the show. So, we started advertising the roast of Imus, and within days the show was a sellout. Big-time celebrities were out for that one. What a memorable night. Imus really enjoyed it. His radio family did a great job of roasting him.

I continued bumping into Imus periodically over the next year or so. I knew that he had some problems with his health, a condition which put him off the jogging paths for awhile, but when he came back, he started working out again. I asked Imus if he would let me honor him with the President's Council on Physical Fitness Award. Who better to honor? He came back from problems with drugs and his health. I think he really appreciated that award and gave quite an acceptance speech that had the crowd going as well. While I don't see Don anymore, he has my respect and admiration for the many charitable fundraising events he continues to do, particularly the creation of The Children's Ranch.

"Rudy is a great man and a great friend. He does things first class, whether it is putting on the Heisman dinner or the widely popular golf tournaments, I always look forward to going to one of Rudy's events."

    —Yogi Berra
      New York Yankees' Hall of Famer

Imagine being in the same room as all of your old heroes. Everyone is eating, drinking and sharing stories. You have men from the first half of the century talking to men in their twenties, and they all are related by a common thread. There is no pretentiousness; everyones' egos are checked at the door. You are able to drift from group to group and carry on a conversation with these men. They demand respect, not with words, but with their bearing. However, they are quick to reciprocate. To a man, they are remarkable. As a group, they are the Heisman Trophy winners.

The Heisman Trophy

Chapter Ten

Very few people have been invited into this group who have not won the award. One man, however, has been an integral part of this group. Although he never played a down of college football, he is linked to the group by the same traditions accompanying the trophy. Each year for the past 40 years, Rudy Riska has been involved in the Heisman Trophy ceremony. As the years progressed, his role has increased to the point where many of the past winners claim Rudy is the glue that holds the group together. The following pages provide a glimpse into this select group through the eyes of Rudy.

How lucky I have been to have the opportunity to be part of a great tradition and American history. Collegiate football's excitement spans the century. The Heisman Trophy and the legends of its winners are an important part of that history. The Heisman is an inspiration to our country's youth, and its traditions are woven into our memories. From the day my father first showed me and my brother the trophy, I became enamored with college football and the Heisman Trophy winners.

In my forty-year association with the Heisman, there have been many changes with the awards process. Initially, the awarding of the Heisman was a one-day affair with a dinner at the Club. Today, the process has evolved into a four-day event that features a television special and a dinner at the New York Marriott Marquis that is attended by over two-thousand people. Even more activities expand beyond the traditional Heisman ceremony in December. For example, the Heisman Foundation, the charity arm of the Heisman winners, and the Downtown Athletic Club have brought the trophy winners together over the years at golf tournaments and other events, allowing the winners to develop a closer bond with each other. The Heisman Foundation itself has helped raise $1.5 million over the past ten years, as well as helped educate people across the country about the Heisman Trophy and its traditions. The Heisman winners are very proud of their association with this program. Archie Griffin, the only two-time Heisman winner, is the national spokesman for the foundation.

1939 HEISMAN WINNER NILES KINNICK RECEIVES HIS AWARD AT A CEREMONY CONDUCTED AT THE CLUB.

DAVE THOMAS (R) CONTINUES TO BE A MAJOR SUPPORTER OF OUR WENDY'S HIGH SCHOOL HEISMAN PROGRAM. DAVE IS SHOWN WITH TWO OHIO STATE HEISMAN TROPHY WINNERS—ARCHIE GRIFFIN (L) AND EDDIE GEORGE (C), ALONG WITH TWO OF THE TALENTED HIGH SCHOOL STUDENT-ATHLETES THAT HAVE BEEN HONORED.

One of the sponsored programs that is conducted with the Heisman ceremonies is the Wendy's National Heisman High School Award held on Friday evening of the awards weekend. This award uses the Heisman as a symbol of excellence and involves over twenty thousand male and female high school seniors every year. Of all the criteria used in choosing the winners of the Wendy's Heisman award, a special emphasis is placed on community service, academics, and athletics. Dave Thomas, the founder of Wendy's who is involved in numerous wonderful charitable causes, is extremely proud of the high school program involving the Heisman. Wendy's staff members, like Don Calhoun, Denny Lynch, Debby Aloway and Pam Camburn, have been invaluable in the successful effort to make the Wendy's award a showcase program.

On the Sunday night before the festivities at the Marriott Marquis, the exclusive pre-Heisman dinner and dance is held at the Club, welcoming the new Heisman winner into the exclusive fraternity. Monday morning the Chase/Tri-State/Madison Square Garden Network high school awards breakfast is held at the club. This program is now in its 17th year and has grown to honor over forty players plus the presentation of a lifetime achievement award to a coach for his career achievements. This awards program was started with the help of Bill Travers, the former scholastic sports editor from the *Daily News*. Today, it falls under the leadership of Mike Quick from MSG television and is ably supported by Andy Parton and Chase Manhattan Bank.

We at the DAC view ourselves as the keepers of the award, and take great efforts to preserve and foster its much deserved reputation these past 67 years. Therefore, any programs run in association with the Heisman Trophy must past the closest scrutiny. Each year, we emphasize these points to the new Heisman Chairman and committee members, so that they better understand the legacy of the award with which they are to be associated. It is these measures that have made the Heisman Trophy one of the premier awards in the world.

Each Heisman Trophy winner is a member of a unique and special group of people. Over the years, it has been obvious to me that the past winners have an immediate influence on the most recent winner. From Jay Berwanger, the first winner in 1935, to Chris Weinke, 2000's winner, each Heisman recipient has given me many wonderful moments to cherish, and I will be forever grateful for their friendship and respect.

When I knew I wasn't going to pitch anymore in the minor leagues, (it was evident that the tendinitis in my shoulder was not going to go away), I took a job selling sporting goods with a friend of mine, Tony Amideo, who ran a store on Nassau Street. Tony had

YALE'S LARRY KELLEY, THE FIRST RECIPIENT OF THE RENAMED HEISMAN TROPHY (JAY BERWANGER WON THE AWARD FIRST — BEFORE IT WAS KNOWN AS THE HEISMAN), SHOWN WITH HIS PROUD MOTHER LOOKING ON, IS PRESENTED HIS AWARD BY THE DAC'S PRESIDENT.

sold some sporting goods to the DAC before and had heard they were starting a basket-ball league. Tony asked if I wanted to come down and work the basketball league part-time. That was in March of 1960 and led to my first experience with the DAC. I subse-quently worked in the DAC gymnasium throughout the summer and fall and was not involved with the Heisman that year because I was only employed part-time. Joe Bellino was the Heisman winner that year.

1944 HEISMAN WINNER
LES HORVATH OF OHIO STATE.

In 1961, when Ernie Davis was the winner, I was responsible for carrying the Heisman trophy up to the Waldorf Astoria hotel, where Ernie was to meet President John F. Kennedy. This was the first direct contact I had with the Heisman and the first winner with whom I had contact. This was somewhat ironic because on the 25th anniversary of Ernie's death, we were doing the Heisman announcement on CBS, and Ed Goren, who was the executive producer for CBS's television special of the Heisman announcement, came up with the idea of honoring Ernie Davis on this occasion. What a wonderful piece Ed put together on Ernie. It was a special moment devoted to a special man.

Mike Noone, a Club member who was a volunteer for the Leukemia Society of America, was so moved by the CBS segment, that he approached me about developing an award named after Ernie to benefit the Leukemia Society of America. Leukemia had taken Ernie from the world far too soon, years earlier. I told them they didn't need permission from the Club if they weren't using the Heisman name, but that they should run it past Ernie's mother. She gave her blessing on creating the award.

I then called a good friend of mine, Dave Hanlon, CEO of Harrah's in Atlantic City, and asked if Harrah's would like to host the Ernie Davis Award at their New Jersey facilities. Because I had done a couple of previous favors for Dave in Atlantic City, he was familiar and comfortable with me. I told him what the award was all about. As a result, Harrah's donated $35,000 to the project, plus all expenses in holding the awards dinner. We formed a committee that in 1986 named Jim Plunkett the first recipient of the Ernie Davis Award. The dinner was held two days after the Heisman ceremonies in order to allow some of the past Heisman winners to stay over and attend.

The great thing about that first Ernie Davis Award dinner was that, unbeknownst to any of us at the DAC, one of Plunkett's former teammates from Stanford, Phil Satre, was now the president of Harrah's and Holiday Inn. Phil had flown in a number of Plunkett's teammates from Stanford. It was a real emotional night, with tears flowing. Not surprisingly, the award became an immediate success. Among the other winners of this award were Joe Paterno and Gale Sayers, two individuals who went on to achieve success, not only in football, but also in society. Over the years, both of these two fine gentlemen have been very active with charities. Today, we're still involved with the Ernie Davis Youth Center up in Elmira, NY.

The following year, I became a full-time employee of the DAC. In time, my role with the Heisman kept expanding to the point where today, to some people, I'm synonymous with the award. I am very proud of such a contention, as well as the complimentary remarks past winners have expressed, following their time with us at the DAC. Am I instrumental in a lot of the things that go with the award? Yes, but I'm not out to take credit for the success of either the Heisman or the winners… the award is the success. But, what I think I have been able to do is to guide and protect the award from people who might try to make money the wrong way on it or by commercializing the dinners. I like to think of myself as the "conscience of the Heisman." I think that past Heisman winners respect me for taking that kind of an interest in the award, even though the Club, because of some recent financial difficulties, has had to try to raise some money through a limited degree of commercialization of the award. Maybe that is just the day and age we live in, and commercialization of everything is inevitable. Personally, I don't know, but if that is the case, we can still do it the right way. I think we've created a situation where

1961 HEISMAN TROPHY
WINNER ERNIE DAVIS MEETS
PRESIDENT JOHN F. KENNEDY
AT THE WALDORF ASTORIA HOTEL.

there is great tradition, great history with the Heisman. There is also great respect for this award. I think the Heisman winners among themselves have coined the idea of an exclusive fraternity. They are proud of it. They are equally proud to help the DAC. They are also proud of the Heisman Foundation and the money we have raised for various charities by utilizing the past Heisman winners as a collective group. And, I am very proud to be a part of it all.

There are hundreds of Heisman highlights and stories involving the 40 years that I have been associated with the award. In the next several pages, I would like to share some of my favorites.

AT A HEISMAN DINNER, FORMER CLUB PRESIDENT BILL BLUM LOOKS OVER THE SHOULDERS OF TWO ICONS OF THE SPORTS WORLD—JOE PATERNO AND YOGI BERRA.

THE MEN WHO CREATED THE HEISMAN

WILLIAM B. PRINCE

Despite the name of the award, the Heisman Trophy's regal past can be traced to royalty—a Prince to be exact. William B. Prince was the individual responsible for the idea of an award honoring the best collegiate football player east of the Mississippi River. Called the DAC Trophy, the award was won by Jay Berwanger of the University of Chicago in 1935.

Prince was an executive with the Downtown Athletic Club when he concocted his famous plan. However, the man was much more than just a collegiate football footnote. William Prince was a man of letters. He graduated from the Boston School of Fine Arts in 1910, and went on to study in England, France, Germany, Italy, Scotland and Switzerland. He was also a war hero, enlisting in the Army soon after World War I broke out in 1917, becoming the first American army man trained in airplane photography map work. For his bravery in battle, Prince was awarded the Verdun Medal and the Silver Star.

After the War, Prince moved to New York City where he worked on house publications for several organizations, the *DAC Journal* among them. He also authored several articles for *American Home* magazine, the American Rose Society and the American Geographic Society. But, his involvement with the DAC and the collegiate award took center stage. As chairman of the award, Prince was the individual responsible for commissioning Frank Eliscu to create the statue that is now the Heisman trophy. He was also the man responsible for gaining John Heisman's support for the initial award won by Berwanger. Finally, he was the driving force behind the award's national acceptance and celebrity.

Prince passed away on September 3, 1949 at the beginning of the collegiate football season that would see Leon Hart win the 15th Heisman Trophy. To the many others who have been in some way connected with the award, William B. Prince can truly claim to be the "Father of the Heisman Trophy."

JOHN W. HEISMAN

In one of the ironies of sports, most people know relatively little about the man whose name adorns the most prestigious award in collegiate football—John W. Heisman, one of the luminaries of the game. His shrewd mind and dedication to the fledgling sport helped shape the game as we know it today.

Heisman played football at two Ivy League schools: Brown and Penn. In 1892, he began his illustrious 36-year coaching career, leading Oberlin College to a perfect record. His coaching stops took him to campuses across the country, including Auburn, Clemson, Georgia Tech, Penn, and Washington and Jefferson. During his coaching career, he introduced innovations that molded the sport of modern football. For example, while scouting a Georgia-North Carolina game in 1895, Heisman saw the Carolina punter throw a ball in desperation when he could not get the kick off. The resulting 70-yard touchdown pass convinced Heisman that the play had a place in the game. Spurred on by the increasing level of roughness in the game that was brought about by such formations as the flying wedge, Heisman petitioned the Rules Committee and its chairman, Walter Camp, to legalize the forward pass. For three years, Heisman's entreaties fell upon deaf ears. Finally, Heisman bypassed Camp, and enlisted two members of the Committee to help his cause. In 1906, the forward pass was legalized.

Another of Heisman's innovations was the "hidden-ball play," a scenario where the ball carrier would tuck the football under his jersey and proceed untouched down the field. This play was quickly outlawed, however. Heisman is also credited by many individuals with originating the center snap in 1893, a full year before Amos Alonzo Stagg was purported to have implemented the play.

The most renowned period of Heisman's involvement with football dates to his sixteen-year stewardship of the Georgia Tech program in the early part of the 20th century. Heisman's Tech teams of 1915-1917 were undefeated, with an astounding record of 25-0. It was during this era that the renowned coach developed the feared offensive formation, the Heisman shift. During this period, Georgia Tech outscored opponents 1,129 to 61. Among the most unforgettable victories achieved by Heisman's Golden Tornadoes was a 222-0 drubbing of Cumberland.

Heisman retired from coaching in 1927 and moved to New York City, where he lived in an apartment on Park Avenue and took up golf. Three years later, he began his association with the Downtown Athletic Club, when he became the Club's first Athletic Director. In 1935, personnel at the DAC conceived the idea for a football award to be given to the best collegiate football player east of the Mississippi River. Ironically, the idea originated with DAC executive William Prince, not Heisman. Heisman gave his support to the award, but denied the club from naming it after him. It was not until his death in 1936 and subsequent burial in Rhinelander, Wisconsin, that the Club executives honored Heisman by naming the award after him. Today, the John W. Heisman memorial trophy links the legendary coach with the game's brightest collegiate stars.

FRANK ELISCU*

While skilled athletes are sometimes compared to artists in their performance, how often is a nationally acclaimed sculptor, one whose works include a national monument and a Presidential medal, who has authored three major books on sculpture technique, and whose work you would be fortunate to have in your home, linked to the very foundation of a great American sporting institution? Frank Eliscu may not be a household name for those who follow football, but he is the individual responsible for the design of the Heisman Trophy.

Eliscu graduated from George Washington High in New York City and Pratt Institute in Brooklyn. He continued his studies at the Beaux-Arts Institute of Design before serving as an apprentice to master sculptor Rudolph Evans. It was under Evans, when Eliscu worked on the Jefferson Memorial in Washington, D.C.

Eliscu was only in his early twenties when he won a National Academy prize for sculpture and when the Heisman Committee selected his designs from a pool of accomplished artist applicants. Eliscu then developed and created the trophy, which was his first commissioned work of art. While his career blossomed after this creation with such works as President Ford's Inaugural medal, a 20-foot panel entitled "Cascade of Books" that is in the Library of Congress building, and his limited-edition designs for Steuben Glass (some of which are priced at more than $40,000 each), Eliscu held a special place in his heart for the trophy he designed. He once wrote, "I have done many large and important commissions since 1935, but the thrill and excitement of doing the Heisman has never been surpassed."

Eliscu and his wife, Mildred, (also a native New Yorker), regularly attended the Heisman Award dinners until their deaths in 1996. And while the ceremonies will not benefit from his physical presence, Frank Eliscu will always be the designer of the Heisman Trophy, forever linking the exceptional artist with the Trophy's distinguished recipients.

* Portions of this story are reprinted with permission from John Prince's article, *"In Memoriam: Frank Eliscu, 1912-1996"*, that originally appeared in the 1997 DAC Journal.

REMINISCING WITH 1973 HEISMAN TROPHY WINNER JOHN CAPPELLETTI AT A RECENT HEISMAN DINNER.

JOHN CAPPELLETTI

What made the 1973 Heisman Awards dinner even more noteworthy was the fact that John's Cappelletti's brother, Joey, who was diagnosed with terminal leukemia, was going for treatments in Philadelphia. And when you go for this particular series of treatments, you stay there for three or four days at a time. Joey would make friends with other kids at the hospital who were also getting treatments. The next time Joey would go to the hospital, he would look for his friends, but they'd be dead. Joey had outlived the time he was supposed to go for treatments, but his parents couldn't bear to tell him that his friends had died. It was a very sad situation.

When John made his speech, with Joey in the audience, he was extremely sincere in his remarks—especially his comments concerning his younger brother. When John's speech was over, everyone in the audience at the Hilton was crying, including President Gerald Ford.

This was definitely a very special occurrence. Archbishop Fulton Sheen then rose to give the benediction, and when he got up, his eyes were like black coals. I was sitting right up front with Joe Torre, and we both noticed it. In his booming voice, the archbishop said, "You have all been blessed by young Cappelletti's words, there is no need for my blessings." And then, as he threw his hands out over the crowd, he said "Dominus Verbiscum!"

When he threw his hands out, everybody's hair went up in the air because of all the electricity in the room. It was a powerful moment to say the least and one of the great moments in Heisman history. The story has been memorialized in the movie *Something for Joey*. John is about as fine a person as you're ever going to find. He has been an active past winner, who has attended a number of our Heisman functions over the years.

BISHOP FULTON SHEEN DURING THE CLOSING REMARKS OF THE 1973 HEISMAN DINNER STATED, "YOU HAVE ALL BEEN BLESSED BY YOUNG CAPPELLETTI'S WORDS, THERE IS NO NEED FOR MY BLESSINGS."

LES HORVATH

There is a great story often told about Les Horvath, the 1944 Heisman winner. Horvath's first wife, Shirley, had recently moved in with him after getting married when she saw the trophy and asked, "What's that?" Les told her what a great honor the Heisman was and how exclusive the award was, trying to help her understand its history and importance. The second week of their marriage, they got invited over to the home of Tommy and Elyse Harmon who lived in Los Angeles. They went, and, of course, she saw a Heisman trophy sitting there, but said nothing.

A couple weeks later they get invited over to Glenn and Harriet Davis' house, and she saw another Heisman trophy sitting in the Davis' house. When they returned home that evening, she proceeded to let Les have it, saying how that trophy obviously wasn't special… since everyone in Los Angeles seemed to have one!

STEVE OWENS

When Steve won the Heisman in 1969, we were still holding the ceremony at the DAC. The night of the awards dinner, Tom Seaver and Howard Cosell were also on the dais with Steve. When John Ott, a former President of the DAC, presented Steve with the award he started to cry. It was such an emotional moment; everybody in the room stood up to applaud. Everybody but Howard Cosell. Howard could be a strange bird at times. I was in charge of the dais that night and was standing nearby when I heard two Irish guys sitting in the front row say, "Look at that prick (referring to Cosell), he won't stand up. Let's get him after the show!" So, I go up to Howard and tell him that a couple of guys took offense to the fact that he didn't stand up when everyone else did and that they were going to try to get him after the show. Of course, Howard complained that it's a free country, and he shouldn't have to stand up if he doesn't want to. I told him that's fine, that I was just trying to help him out.

Eventually, I got Howard out through the back door to the elevator. In those days, we had an elevator operator who opened and shut the elevator's gate. Just as the guy closed the gate, one of the angry Irishmen threw a punch at Howard, just missing the startled Cosell. As we were going down in the elevator someone asked Howard if he wanted to stop off at the third floor for a nightcap, which was customary for the celebrities to do. Howard told him, 'no, he had an important meeting to get to.' When the elevator hit the lobby, Howard ran out of there more quickly than I had ever seen him move!

The next day, Steve wanted to take his mother and father out to a nice restaurant. I had started sort of a tradition where I would take the Heisman winner to my favorite restaurant in Little Italy. Steve and I were going to meet up with his parents at the restaurant, after running uptown to do the Johnny Carson show, which in those days was taped at 6 p.m. in New York. So, off we went with the trophy to the Carson show. When we got to the green room, there was none other than Muhammad Ali, who at the time I wasn't real crazy about because of his efforts to dodge the draft and all that. Now, as I grow older, I'm able to see other people's perspectives a little better, but at that time I didn't care much for a guy who wouldn't fight for his country. I didn't want to call him Muhammad Ali, so I called him Cassius as I introduced Steve and myself. Muhammad was there to promote a Broadway play that he was in at the time.

Steve's turn came up, and out he went to meet with Johnny. As he was being interviewed, in came an intern asking for Steve Owens, saying there was a call from

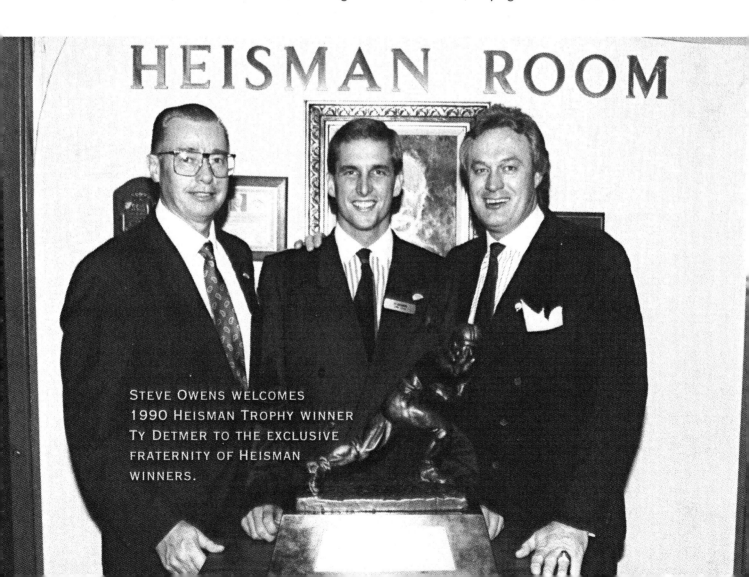

STEVE OWENS WELCOMES
1990 HEISMAN TROPHY WINNER
TY DETMER TO THE EXCLUSIVE
FRATERNITY OF HEISMAN
WINNERS.

HEISMAN ROOM

SHARING A LAUGH WITH FORMER L.A. DODGERS MANAGER TOMMY LASORDA, HOWARD COSELL WAS IN A MUCH BETTER MOOD THAN HE WAS DURING THE 1969 HEISMAN DINNER. HE GOT CHASED OUT OF THE DAC BY A COUPLE OF GUYS WHO WERE ANGRY HE DIDN'T STAND UP WITH THE REST OF THE CROWD WHEN STEVE OWENS WAS PRESENTED THE AWARD. HOWARD WAS CERTAINLY ONE OF A KIND.

Washington for him. I told the kid he can't talk now, he was doing the show, but that I would take the call. I then got on the phone, and it was an aide for President Nixon, checking to see if Steve wanted to fly with the President the next day to attend the Texas-Arkansas football game. I got a number, and said Steve would call back. Steve got done with Carson, and we headed to the restaurant, figuring Steve could call the President from there. Of course, the phone in the restaurant didn't work, so I told Steve let's go down around the corner to the drugstore and call from the phone booth there. That particular phone booth didn't have a door. When Steve then dialed the number and asked for President Nixon, the whole place stopped, looked and listened. It was like an EF Hutton commercial!

Steve made the call, and we headed back to the restaurant. I told Steve to take the trophy with him on his trip. I then gave him a set of cufflinks that I had made so he would have something to give the President as a gift. The next day on the news, they showed Steve giving President Nixon his cufflinks and the President giving Steve his. It was unbelievable! Without question, Steve has been a great ambassador for the Heisman Trophy and a great friend to me personally over the years.

Regardless of your current impression of O.J. Simpson, he is a Heisman winner. Personally, the O.J. I like to remember is the twenty-one year old kid who came through the DAC doors in 1968, not exactly sure what was happening to him.

Normally, the announcement of the Heisman winner would occur on a Friday, while the Heisman awards program and dinner would then be held the next Wednesday and Thursday. O.J. came to New York City four days early to do the Ed Sullivan Show on a Sunday night. The sports information director at USC told O.J. to contact the Club rather than fly back to California, and, then two days later, turn around and fly back to New York for the Heisman presentation. When he was scheduled to head down to the DAC, he erroneously told the cab driver to take him to the New York Athletic Club. Of course they were pleased O.J. showed up there, but quickly realized the mistake he had made and gave me a call at the DAC.

I was requested to host O.J. during the days leading up to the presentation activities. The first thing the Heisman chairman set up was to pick up a tuxedo for O.J. at a tailor located in Bay Ridge, Brooklyn. Since I had just moved to the same area, after the fitting, we stopped by my house where O.J. met my family and some of my neighbors.

Back at the Club, O.J. told me he was invited to attend the National Football Foundation dinner on Tuesday as a guest of ABC-TV and Roone Arledge. He asked if I was going to be attending that banquet, and I said no. O.J. called the ABC office and requested an invitation for me. Before we left for that dinner, I asked O.J. which of his family members were going to be coming to New York for the Heisman presentation. O.J. either did not know his family members could attend, or he had forgotten to plan for them to come. O.J. told me that his dad really wasn't part of the family, and that his mother and sister may not have the appropriate clothes to wear. I told him that it was more important that his family be in attendance to share his honor of winning the Heisman Trophy. I then got the phone number of his mother in San Francisco and invited her to the presentation, assuring her that I would make all the necessary arrangements. O.J. then got on the phone and began to cry. After this call, he told me his sister would also like to come. Marge Koenig (the executive secretary at the Club for over 45 years) was called and told to make the arrangements. Looking back on it now, I appreciate the trust O.J.'s mother put in me. Here I was calling from the other side of the country, asking her to pack up some things and head to the airport on a moment's notice. I know O.J. really appreciated what we did to make sure they could be there for his big night.

O.J. and his wife were also expecting their first child at this time, so we needed to obtain all the phone numbers where O.J. could be reached. That night, we went to the National Football Foundation dinner and sat with all the executives from ABC-TV, including Howard Cosell. The Tuesday evening after the Hall of Fame dinner, I took O.J. to Forlini's in Little Italy for some linguini with white clam sauce which he had never eaten before.

The next day, Wednesday, a full day of interviews was set up for O.J., concluding with the Club's dinner that was held at the renowned 21 Club. While he was being interviewed for the Fran Tarkenton show, the call finally came that O.J. was the father of a baby girl. Fran had an exclusive! I was scheduled to drop O.J. off at the 21 Club that night. We arrived at the same time as the President of the DAC. O.J. insisted that I attend that night's dinner, which I did not want to do. The President ordered me to stay, and when I told him about O.J. being a new father, he authorized me to buy two boxes of cigars for the reception. When we got to the reception room, I was told to introduce O.J. and give the news of his daughter's birth. Later that evening, his mother and sister arrived, and the evening brought many tears of joy to the family.

After the Heisman awards dinner on Thursday, O.J. asked if I would take him, his mom and sister to the restaurant in Little Italy for linguini and white clam sauce. Apparently, O.J. had been raving about the stuff, and his mother and sister weren't leaving New York without trying it. We ended up getting a big group to head over to Forlini's, led by the New York Fire Commissioner who had his sirens blasting the whole way there. It was quite a sight. We stayed until 4 a.m. and had a fabulous night. Since then, whenever O.J. and I were at a function together, he always made a point of getting up and saying something nice about me. He was always appreciative of the little things we did for him and his family while they stayed with us.

In 1999, during a stay at NYU hospital, I received a call. I asked who it was, and the

1968 HEISMAN TROPHY WINNER O.J. SIMPSON WITH HIS SISTER AND MOTHER AT FORLINI'S IN LITTLE ITALY, WAITING TO TRY SOME LINGUINI AND WHITE CLAM SAUCE "THE JUICE" HAD BEEN RAVING ABOUT TO THEM.

voice on the other end said, "Get out of bed, lazy." It was O.J. We talked for about five minutes and then hung up. I told the nurse that that was O.J. Simpson calling. The next day the same nurse was accompanying a doctor on rounds. When they came to my room she pointed at me and said, "That's the guy who spoke with O.J." The doctor looked at me in disbelief. I think he thought I was taking too much medication! Unfortunately and somewhat inexplicably, the entire O.J. Simpson saga is a tragedy for everyone involved.

EDDIE GEORGE

Eddie George was the fantastic running back from Ohio State who won the 1995 Heisman Trophy. Eddie wanted to leave early the next morning after the Heisman dinner, because a relatively large reception with his teammates was awaiting him back in Columbus. As it turned out, Eddie left so early that morning that he didn't get the trophy's traveling case. He was all set to make the flight back to Columbus. He even had a seat assigned on the plane right next to him for the trophy!

Later that day, the Ohio State Sports Information Director called me and said that airport security had made Eddie run the trophy through the x-ray baggage scanner. When Eddie did this one of the fingers on the trophy broke off. Eddie was in shock. They tried to repair it, but to no avail. Finally, the DAC had another trophy made for Eddie. To this day, I still have Eddie George's broken Heisman trophy sitting in my office.

JIM PLUNKETT

In 1970, the call was made to the President of Stanford University to arrange for Jim Plunkett to be available for the official notification of his winning the Heisman award and for some press interviews. On the Friday that we made the call, we were surprised to find out that Jim was not in California but in New York taping a show for ABC-TV. A call was made, and I was dispatched to the ABC studio to bring Jim to the DAC. College football guru, Beano Cook, rode with Jim and I. When we entered the Club lobby, we were beset by television cameras and newspaper people. We had to hastily set up a room for the expanded press conference. Later, realizing the impact of having the winner available for the announcement, the Club altered policy to always try to have the winner present.

Following the Heisman Awards presentation night, Jim and his Stanford co-captain, Jack Schultz, stayed in the Club for the weekend. On that Friday, arrangements were made for the two to attend a Broadway show. I was to meet them afterwards for a late dinner at Ponte's (Joe Ponte was the Club member who chaired the annual "Salute to Boxing Greats" dinners and who would also host the college boxing teams at a post-fight party in his restaurant). During dinner, Jim and Jack noticed an impressive painting of a beautiful nude woman hanging in the bar area and asked if they could have their photo taken with that painting. Someone in the crowd joked that if they would win the Rose Bowl game they were scheduled to play in, they would get the painting, worth thousands, as a gift. At the time, Stanford was a 17-point underdog to Ohio State.

Sid Gilmore, the Vice President of Sales for Golden West Broadcasting whom I had met through my friend Duke Llewellyn, attended the 1970 Heisman dinner and arranged

PETE DAWKINS, JOHN WAYNE, JIM PLUNKETT, AND MICHAEL WAYNE.
"THE DUKE" WAS A BIG FOOTBALL FAN AND EAGERLY ACCEPTED AN INVITATION
TO ATTEND THE 1971 HEISMAN DINNER.

for me to be a guest of Golden West at the Rose Bowl. Following Stanford's upset of Ohio State, Jim and Jack reminded me of the offer from the patrons at Ponte's. When I got back to New York, I visited Joe and told him the Stanford boys were inquiring about the painting. Joe said he would look into it. A few days later, Joe called to say he would give Jim the painting provided Jim appear in person to pick it up at a special luncheon Joe was planning. I called Jim with the news.

Jim was scheduled to come out east in February for the Walter Camp award, but said he would arrange his trip to come a few days earlier. The week Jim was supposed to come east was also the week of the NFL draft and the DAC's annual "All Sports Night" dinner. Jim was scheduled to arrive on Tuesday evening and wanted his stay to be relatively low profile. I was scheduled to pick him up at the airport, but on Tuesday afternoon, I received a call from William Sullivan, the owner of the New England Patriots and the franchise with the first pick in the NFL draft. Mr. Sullivan wanted to talk to Jim, presumably to get some kind of bearing on Jim as a person. So, I asked Mr. Sullivan to pick up Jim at the airport, and then join us for dinner at Ponte's. We had a great dinner that night. Mr. Sullivan was impressed with Jim (as well as with the painting). Mr. Sullivan subsequently stated that the Patriots would select Jim with their number one pick in the next day's draft.

The next morning, I went to Jim's room, and the phones were ringing off the hook as word spread that Jim was in New York and would become the first player chosen in the NFL draft. Mr. Sullivan called and asked if Jim could come uptown immediately following the luncheon at Ponte's. We responded that of course he would.

Pete Rozelle, the NFL Commissioner, then called and told us he wanted Jim at the hotel where the draft was being held. Jim took the call and explained to Commissioner Rozelle about the luncheon at Ponte's and said he wished to honor his obligation. He also added that if the NFL had wanted him to attend the draft, they should have made arrangements with him beforehand. Pete then spoke to me, informing me that we would get no publicity for the Ponte's luncheon. I quickly advised him that it was not a publicity event, but a private and special presentation to Jim. Before we left for the restaurant, we heard the news that Jim was selected by the Patriots with the number one pick of the draft. Mr. Sullivan called Jim at the Club to congratulate him and inform him that he would be coming to the Ponte's luncheon with a group of family and friends.

AL HELFER, THE LEGENDARY SPORTSCASTER AND EMCEE FOR MANY HEISMAN DINNERS, WITH 1970 HEISMAN TROPHY WINNER JIM PLUNKETT.

When we got to Ponte's at noon, it was a media circus. There were trucks from all the networks, and inside the restaurant were Frank Gifford of CBS, Kyle Rote of NBC, and Howard Cosell of ABC, along with many of the top New York newsmen. The luncheon turned into one gigantic press conference, but no one was offended, and a substitute painting (not the nude) was presented to Jim. Howard Cosell could not understand why Jim would be so impressed with the painting. If Howard had seen the nude, he would have understood.

The next day, Jim attended the DAC's All Sports dinner. Having the Heisman winner and number one pick of the NFL made the night unbelievable. Jim says that to this day, the painting still hangs in his fraternity house at Stanford. Jim is an exceptional man, and both he and his wife, Gerry, make many of the Heisman functions during the year.

JIM PLUNKETT GETS SOME TIPS ON HITTING THE LONG BALL FROM YOGI BERRA AND GENE MICHAELS AT YANKEE STADIUM.

1956 HEISMAN TROPHY WINNER PAUL HORNUNG SHARES A MOMENT WITH HIS MOTHER AFTER BECOMING THE FIFTH PLAYER FROM NOTRE DAME TO WIN THE AWARD. NOTRE DAME WENT 2-8 DURING THE 1956 SEASON, BUT HORNUNG HAD A STELLAR YEAR MAKING HIM THE ONLY WINNER TO PLAY ON A LOSING TEAM. PAUL WAS ONE OF THE GREATEST ALL-AROUND FOOTBALL PLAYERS AND WENT ON TO A DISTINGUISHED PRO CAREER ON THE GREAT VINCE LOMBARDI LED GREEN BAY PACKER CHAMPIONSHIP TEAMS.

1972 HEISMAN TROPHY WINNER JOHNNY RODGERS RECEIVES THE AWARD FROM DAC PRESIDENT NEIL MCALISTER.

JOHNNY RODGERS LIKED THE DAC SO MUCH HE ENDED UP GETTING MARRIED AT THE CLUB A NUMBER OF YEARS LATER.

1997 HEISMAN TROPHY WINNER CHARLES WOODSON RECEIVES HIS AWARD FROM DAC PRESIDENT PETER JUNGE. CHARLES HAD AN UNBELIEVABLE 1997 SEASON AT DEFENSIVE BACK, WHILE ALSO MAKING SOME BIG PLAYS ON OFFENSE, TO LEAD MICHIGAN TO THE ROSE BOWL AND A SHARE OF THE NATIONAL TITLE.

WITH HIS FIRST WIFE, 1948 HEISMAN TROPHY WINNER DOAK WALKER ARRIVES IN NEW YORK FOR THE HEISMAN FESTIVITIES. A QUIET GENTLEMAN, DOAK WAS ONE OF THE GREATS IN COLLEGE AND PROFESSIONAL FOOTBALL. HIS SECOND WIFE, SKEETER, AND HER BROTHER, BUDDY WERNER, WERE BOTH OLYMPIC SKIERS. DOAK DIED TRAGICALLY IN A SKI ACCIDENT ON HIS HOMETOWN SLOPES OF STEAMBOAT SPRINGS, COLORADO. DOAK AND HIS LEGEND WILL LIVE ON AS HIS NAME IS ON A NATIONAL AWARD PRESENTED ANNUALLY TO THE OUTSTANDING COLLEGIATE RUNNING BACK.

1977 HEISMAN TROPHY WINNER EARL CAMPBELL WITH HIS PROUD MOTHER AT THE HEISMAN DINNER.

1962 HEISMAN TROPHY WINNER TERRY BAKER OF OREGON STATE WITH DAC PRESIDENT FRANK BARRY AND BOBBY KENNEDY.

1985 HEISMAN TROPHY WINNER VINCENT "BO" JACKSON. BO STUNNED THE SPORTS WORLD WITH HIS OUTSTANDING PERFORMANCES IN THE NFL AND MAJOR LEAGUE BASEBALL. ONE CAN ONLY SPECULATE AT WHAT RECORDS HE WOULD HAVE SET IF HIS CAREER WAS NOT CUT SHORT BY INJURY. BO'S IMPACT ON THE COUNTRY IS STILL FELT AS HE TOURS THE NATION FOR *HEALTH SOUTH*, TALKING TO HIGH SCHOOL STUDENTS ON THE IMPORTANCE OF FITNESS AND HEALTH PROGRAMS.

1999 HEISMAN WINNER RON DAYNE ON THE DAIS AT THE MARRIOTT MARQUIES DURING THE HEISMAN DINNER.

1947 HEISMAN TROPHY WINNER JOHN LUJACK WITH DAC PRESIDENT WILBUR JURDEN. LUJACK FILLED IN FOR ANGELO BERTELLI WHEN ANGELO WAS IN THE MARINES. JOHNNY HAD BEEN DRAFTED AND HAD FULFILLED HIS SERVICE DUTY IN TIME TO RETURN FOR THE 1946 SEASON. HE PLAYED IN THAT MEMORABLE ARMY-NOTRE DAME GAME AT YANKEE STADIUM THAT ENDED IN A 0-0 TIE. TWO VERY PROMINENT PLAYS OF THAT GAME FEATURED JOHNNY AND DOC BLANCHARD. THAT GAME WAS ALSO THE ONLY GAME THAT FEATURED FOUR HEISMAN WINNERS: DOC BLANCHARD, GLENN DAVIS, JOHNNY LUJACK AND THE 1949 WINNER, LEON HART.

COACH AND PLAYER: 1966 HEISMAN TROPHY WINNER STEVE SPURRIER WITH HIS FORMER PLAYER AND 1996 HEISMAN TROPHY WINNER DANNY WUERFFEL.

1988 HEISMAN TROPHY WINNER BARRY SANDERS WAS AN UNHERALDED PLAYER PRIOR TO THE 1988 SEASON. HIS WINNING THE AWARD WAS REMARKABLE IN LIGHT OF THE FACT THAT OKLAHOMA STATE'S GAMES WERE NOT OFTEN TELEVISED NATIONALLY. BARRY TURNED IN A GREAT SEASON, SETTING 25 NCAA RECORDS WHILE AVERAGING 200 YARDS PER GAME. BARRY COULDN'T ATTEND THE PROGRAM WHERE WE ANNOUNCED THAT HE HAD WON THE AWARD BECAUSE HIS TEAM WAS PLAYING THEIR FINAL GAME IN TOKYO, JAPAN.

TIM BROWN BECAME THE SEVENTH HEISMAN TROPHY WINNER FROM NOTRE DAME IN 1987. ALL SIX OF THE PREVIOUS NOTRE DAME WINNERS WERE ON HAND TO WITNESS TIM RECEIVING THE AWARD. THEIR PRESENCE REALLY MADE IT A SPECIAL NIGHT.

1998 HEISMAN WINNER RICKY WILLIAMS WITH 1935 HEISMAN WINNER JAY BERWANGER. ALL OF THE PAST HEISMAN WINNERS LOOKED FORWARD TO SEEING JAY EACH YEAR AT THE HEISMAN DINNER.

1945-47 HEISMAN WINNERS: GLENN DAVIS—ARMY (1946),
JOHN LUJACK—NOTRE DAME (1947), FELIX "DOC"
BLANCHARD—ARMY (1945).

"MR. OUTSIDE"—
1946 HEISMAN WINNER,
GLENN DAVIS.

My first football heroes were "Mr. Inside" and "Mr. Outside," the 1945 and 1946 Heisman winners from West Point, Doc Blanchard and Glenn Davis. As a youngster, my friends and I attended the movie, *The Spirit of West Point,* highlighting the career of the two Army greats. Leaving the theater we ran and tackled each other all the way home. From that day on, I became a lifetime Army football fan. During my duties as Athletic Director, we developed a great relationship between the handball club of the DAC and the officers and cadets of West Point. The events we arranged were not only competition on the courts, but opportunities for family socializing. My dreams were realized as an Army fan when I was able to visit West Point and make friends with people like Art Johnson, Colonel Al Rushatz and Jim and Sue Peterson.

DAVIS (L) AND BLANCHARD (R) WERE PART OF ONE OF THE GREATEST BACKFIELDS IN THE HISTORY OF THE GAME.

"MR. INSIDE"—1945 HEISMAN WINNER, DOC BLANCHARD.

Plus, I was able to develop friendships with Doc, Glenn, and the 1958 Heisman winner, Pete Dawkins. These relationships are very special to me and bring back many fond memories.

1990 HEISMAN TROPHY WINNER TY DETMER WON THE AWARD THAT YEAR AS A JUNIOR, ACHIEVING AN HONOR THAT PREVIOUS GREAT QUARTERBACKS AT BYU COULD NOT ACCOMPLISH. IT IS MY PERSONAL BELIEF THAT TY HAD AN EVEN BETTER SENIOR SEASON, BUT EARLY-SEASON LOSSES TO PENN STATE AND MIAMI ULTIMATELY DOOMED HIS REPEAT CHANCES.

1951 HEISMAN TROPHY WINNER RICHARD KAZMAIER WITH DAC PRESIDENT JOHN POSTELL. KAZMAIER, A PRINCETON GRAD, IS THE LAST WINNER FROM AN IVY LEAGUE SCHOOL. DICK WENT ON TO BECOME ONE OF THE DIRECTORS OF THE NATIONAL FOOTBALL FOUNDATION AND COLLEGE HALL OF FAME. IN 1993, HE RECEIVED THE HALL'S PRESTIGIOUS "DISTINGUISHED AMERICAN AWARD."

1949 HEISMAN TROPHY WINNER LEON HART WAS THE THIRD PLAYER FROM NOTRE DAME TO WIN THE AWARD. HE WAS ALSO THE SECOND LINEMAN TO EVER WIN THE AWARD. LEON ALSO STARRED IN THE NFL.

1980 Heisman Trophy winner George Rogers, with Jim Costello (L), who was the Chairman of the Heisman Trophy Committee that year, and Carmine Ragucci.

1992 Heisman Trophy winner Gino Torretta. Following his NFL career, Gino has begun a career as a college football announcer with ESPN.

1940 winner Tom Harmon in front of his plane. Tom was one of a group of Heisman winners who fought in World War II. Tom had some heroic moments in that conflict. Tom later became the voice of the Heisman dinners with the passing of the legendary Al Helfer. Tom loved the award and his fellow winners. Those feelings came through in his duties as emcee.

THE 2000 HEISMAN FINALISTS: (L-R) LaDAINIAN TOMLINSON, DREW BREES, CHRIS WEINKE (THE WINNER), AND JOSH HEUPEL.

1981 HEISMAN TROPHY WINNER MARCUS ALLEN.

1976 HEISMAN TROPHY WINNER TONY DORSETT DELIVERING HIS ACCEPTANCE SPEECH.

1950 HEISMAN TROPHY WINNER VIC JANOWICZ.

1983 HEISMAN FINALISTS: BYU'S STEVE YOUNG, NEBRASKA'S MIKE ROZIER (THE WINNER), AND BOSTON COLLEGE'S DOUG FLUTIE.

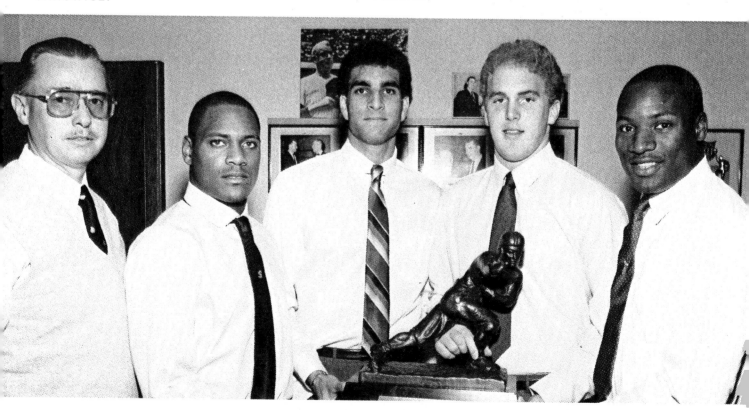

THE 1985 HEISMAN FINALISTS: MICHIGAN STATE'S LORENZO WHITE, MIAMI'S VINNY TESTEVERDE, IOWA'S CHUCK LONG, AND THE WINNER — AUBURN'S BO JACKSON.

40 YEARS AT THE HOME OF THE HEISMAN

The exclusive fraternity of former Heisman winners grows by one each year. The college football player fortunate enough to win the award will join that exclusive fraternity and in doing so, will take part in one of the most memorable nights of his young life. In this chapter, past Heisman winners recount the events of their stay while in New York City for their Heisman Trophy presentation.

For some, it was the first time they had ever been on a plane. For others, it was the first time they ever came to New York. But for all, it was a memory that would last them a lifetime.

What the Heisman has Meant to Me

Chapter Eleven

ROGER STAUBACH IN 1963, WITH CARMEN RAGUCCI, CHAIRMAN OF THE
HEISMAN TROPHY COMMITTEE.

ROGER STAUBACH, NAVY, 1963

The season during which Roger Staubach won the Heisman award, he was not thinking about garnering national recognition. Staubach was coming off a successful sophomore year, when he had moved ahead of four upper-class quarterbacks to start the final four games for the Naval Academy. The next year, it was the Academy's athletic PR person, Bud Tollman, who realized Staubach's potential for an award like the Heisman. Tollman made sure that Roger was visible to media representatives, putting him on the cover of the team's press guide. While this pales in comparison to the full-blown publicity machines that often accompany many of the current group of Heisman hopefuls, Tollman's efforts, in conjunction with Staubach's outstanding play, earned Staubach the reputation as one of the nation's premier collegiate football players.

Staubach had unconsciously been linked to the Heisman since his boyhood days growing up in Silverton, Ohio. As a young man, he had closely followed the exploits of fellow Heisman winners, individuals like Hopalong Cassady at Ohio State, Alan Ameche at Wisconsin, and Glenn Davis at Army to name a few. And it was the exploits of another Heisman-winning Midshipman, Joe Bellino, that led Staubach to choose the Naval Academy over the numerous scholarship offers he had received from the geographically closer Big Ten schools.

A running quarterback in high school, Staubach spent one year at The New Mexico Military Institute in Roswell, New Mexico before matriculating to Annapolis. It was in Roswell where he began to develop the accuracy and arm strength that became his trademark throughout his collegiate and professional career.

Roger found out about winning the award while sitting in the Navy locker room, when USNA head coach Wayne Hardin made the announcement in front of the team. There was obvious excitement among his Midshipmen teammates. Ever the team player, Roger vowed to chop up the Heisman Trophy and send each teammate a piece—a promise that has yet to be fulfilled, but one that Roger is reminded of from time to time by teammates.

According to Staubach, "The mood in Silverton was ecstatic. It was a big deal to my parents, since I was the only child. My mother worked at the General Motors plant where she and everyone else was very proud."

Staubach, his parents, and his girlfriend, (whom he eventually married) all made the trip to New York City for the Heisman Trophy dinner. Because it was Roger's first time to the Big Apple, it was arranged for him to take in a Broadway show. The group was waiting in the theater lobby before the performance, when theatergoers began to hand Roger their tickets. Since he was dressed in his Navy uniform, Roger surmised that they thought that he was an usher.

Despite the lack of recognition in the theater district, Staubach has fond memories of the awards dinner. One special memory was the speech given by his father. The Heisman people asked his dad to get up and say a few words. He was a diabetic and was really struggling at the time. But, he got up there and gave the speech. Roger remembers one of the things his father said was, "God gave us one child, and he gave us a good one." Roger could really see the pride in his father's face during that speech.

Staubach's successes after leaving the Navy are no secret. He had an outstanding professional career, complete with Super Bowl championships and an induction into the NFL's Hall of Fame. He is also a very successful businessman, running a real estate company in Dallas. But yet, Staubach is never far removed from his Heisman Trophy award. According to Roger, it's funny, he never would have dreamed of winning all those awards and championships. But today, whenever he is introduced at a function, formal or informal, the two phrases that are always used are: Heisman Trophy winner and NFL Hall of Famer.

Like other men of his day, Staubach remains modest of his athletic successes. For example, he tries to keep all the football memorabilia out of his office. Keep in mind that he runs a relatively large company that is located in an 80,000-square foot building. A lot of people come to his office wanting to see his awards, particularly the Heisman. But he keeps his Heisman Trophy at home, where his wife has designed a room for his awards.

No matter who you are, there are fantastic memories associated with the Heisman award. As for being one of the members of the select Heisman fraternity, Staubach feels privileged to part of the family. "The Heisman is associated with so many people, and it becomes a part of your life. There is no other award that has that type of association. You become bonded to other winners, even if you do not know them personally. And the winners that you do know personally, the relationship is even more special. Winning the award has been a fantastically positive experience."

To this day, Staubach still keeps in touch with other Heisman winners. He got to know Alan Ameche's wife, and through her, Glenn Davis. The Heisman Trophy is particularly important to the service academies. At the 100th anniversary of the Army-Navy game, Pete Dawkins, Doc Blanchard, Joe Bellino and Roger were in attendance. He also occasionally gets together with Gary Beban, who is also a successful real estate businessman. Along with Steve Owens, Tony Dorsett, and Earl Campbell, he is an integral part of the Texas Heisman connection. He also has a unique connection to O.J. Simpson, since they were the first Heisman Trophy winners to be inducted into the NFL Hall of Fame. It is little wonder that every Heisman winner feels such an emotional attachment to the "Heisman fraternity."

When discussing his experiences with Rudy Riska, Staubach echoes the sentiments of many former Heisman winners. "Rudy is the glue that has kept the Heisman Trophy together. He is the link that keeps all the winners together. He is a great guy with a tremendous respect for the Heisman Trophy and what it stands for. With all the marketing opportunities that are available, you really have to be careful in how you treat the award, and Rudy has done that. Plus, Rudy has really kept the history of the award together."

—Roger Staubach

(L-R) IRV CROSS, 1989 HEISMAN TROPHY WINNER ANDRE WARE, AND 1963 HEISMAN TROPHY WINNER ROGER STAUBACH.

BOTH BELLINO AND STAUBACH ENJOY RETURNING TO THE DAC FOR HEISMAN
FOUNDATION ACTIVITIES THROUGHOUT THE YEAR. (L-R) CARMINE RAGUCCI,
STEVE OWENS, ANGELO BERTELLI, A NORTHWESTERN UNIVERSITY
REPRESENTATIVE, DANNY WUERFFEL, ROGER STAUBACH, SAL SCHILIRO
AND JOE BELLINO.

JOE BELLINO, NAVY, 1960

The great Naval Academy running back, Joe Bellino, won the Heisman Trophy for his on-the-field exploits as his Cinderella Navy team upset many teams, including then top-ranked Washington. But not surprisingly, one of Bellino's earliest memories associated with the Heisman Award centers around academics.

According to Joe, "At the time, my main priority was graduating from the Naval Academy, rather than winning any college football awards. Academics were first with me, then football, and I was having difficulty in my electrical engineering class. At the time of the Heisman announcement, I remember being in that class when the watch officer came into the room and told the professor that the school superintendent wanted to see me immediately. I thought I was in big trouble for failing the class, and that I would be expelled from school. When I went into his office, he was there with the SID, John Cox, and head coach Wayne Hardin. The superintendent told me that he had just received a telegram from the DAC informing him that I had won that year's Heisman Trophy award. My first reaction wasn't to jump in the air, but I just said, 'Thank God!' because I thought I was failing the class, and they were going to kick me out of school [Bellino subsequently passed the course comfortably].

"The AP reporters then came into the office to interview me. They asked, "Joe, you have earned All-American honors, won the Maxwell Award for being the nation's out-standing player and now the Heisman. Is there anything else you would like to do?"

Bellino, a Massachusetts native, replied, "There's another gentleman from Massachusetts who has had a pretty good year, and I would like to meet him." He was, of course, talking about President-elect John F. Kennedy. The next day in the papers, the headlines reiterated Bellino's request: "Bellino wins Heisman, wants to meet Kennedy." That day, Joe got a telegram from the President asking him to come to the White House.

Reflecting upon what winning the Heisman Trophy has meant to him, Bellino fully recognizes the impact that the Heisman has had on his life.

1960 HEISMAN TROPHY WINNER JOE BELLINO WITH DAC PRESIDENT CLIFF DEMING.

"As the list of the winners' names grows, I am proud to be a member of such a select group. When I am in groups with professional athletes who have won other championships, Super Bowl rings, NBA Championship rings, etc., everyone looks at it [the Heisman ring] in awe. We are a very select group. When we win it, we all say the same things. We thank our parents, our teammates, and our school. That hasn't changed. What has changed is the effect it has had on my family. All the hundreds of nieces and nephews and cousins can say, 'My uncle won the Heisman Trophy,' or 'my dad won the

Heisman Trophy." The importance of my winning the award for my family and teammates has grown over the years. My teammates have been bragging about it for 40 years.

"When I won the award, I was worried about exams. You win all the awards, but don't put things in perspective. Forty years later, the importance is amplified one-hundred fold. You will be a Heisman Trophy winner for the rest of your life. We are part of the history of the game and of our school. It means a lot to the Naval Academy."

When asked to offer advice to recent winners of the Heisman, Bellino comments, "Regardless of how well an individual does, he will be judged twenty, thirty, forty years from now on how he has handled himself in life. Heisman winners are so busy from when they win it for the next twenty-five years—wrapped up in business, athletics, etc. But 25 years later, you look and say, 'What's important?' Now, at the dinners you see the old-timers, because they know what's important. It behooves the winners to toe the mark. They effect thousands of people, and if they don't live up to the integrity of the Heisman Award, shame on them."

Bellino credits Rudy with enhancing the brotherhood of Heisman winners. "The last 15 years, I have gotten to know Rudy, once I started to go back to the ceremony. If you call all the guys, they will tell you that Rudy has been the focal point of maintaining the integrity of the individuals who win the Heisman. Rudy has been the glue that has held the group together. He has been able to talk to us individually and bond the winners as a group. By getting us involved in charity events, by guiding us as individuals, Rudy leads us in the proper direction. Without a person like Rudy, you would not be in contact with the other winners. He has kept the fraternity together. Today, when I get a call from someone saying that they got my name from the DAC, I call Rudy and his staff, and they tell me what's going on. Then, I'm happy to help out because I know that if Rudy okayed it, it will be good for us as a group."

ROGER & ME

"Roger Staubach and I have a special bond on several levels. First, we both graduated from the Academy. There is always some bond between Academy graduates. There is also the Heisman Trophy bond. The Academy uses this. They call us in to appear at big games, or at pep rallies. I owe a lot to the Academy and am happy to give back in this way. Roger and I also have another bond. I graduated from the Academy when Roger first entered school. I stayed around one year to coach the backfield on the plebe team where Roger was the quarterback. There was a good picture in *Sport* magazine not too long back with me showing the plebe backfield how to hold the ball, and Roger was one of the three plebes standing there.

"At the end of that season, the varsity coaches and the plebe coaches sat down to discuss personnel. The head coach had Roger penciled in as a halfback. Roger had an accurate arm, but he really couldn't throw a tight spiral, like you see Marino or Elway do. His passes wobbled, but they got there. Well, the coach thought he was a running back. I told him, 'No Way! Staubach is your quarterback.'

"Today, I joke with Roger that the only reason I did that was so he wouldn't break all my records. He was a heckuva runner."

—Joe Bellino

HOWARD A. "HOPALONG" CASSADY, OHIO STATE, 1955

Howard Cassady, the great Ohio State player, won the Heisman award in 1955, one year after finishing as the runner up to another Big 10 star, Alan Ameche, despite the fact that Cassady won the 1954 Big 10 MVP award.

Cassady recalled first hearing about winning the award from none other than George Steinbrenner. Cassady had met Steinbrenner when he was going through his flight training at Lockbourne Air Force base in Columbus, Ohio, where Steinbrenner was the football and baseball coach. Cassady then moved on to Ohio State. In 1955, Steinbrenner was the offensive coordinator at Northwestern. The day before the announcement was supposed to air, Steinbrenner called Cassady and said, "Hop, my sources tell me that you are going to win the Heisman Trophy." The next day, the announcement came out, proving Steinbrenner right.

1955 HEISMAN TROPHY WINNER HOWARD "HOPALONG" CASSADY POSES WITH THE AWARD. HOP AND HIS WIFE, BARBARA, ARE PART OF THE REGULARS WHO RETURN EACH YEAR FOR THE HEISMAN CELEBRATION.

Cassady feels that the general level of excitement concerning the Heisman was somewhat muted, when compared to the current situation. In fact, he says, "Compared to what it [the Heisman experience] is now, there wasn't much when I won it."

Cassady left Columbus the morning of the award presentation with a diverse group of individuals that included Harry Strobel (the line coach at Ohio State who was substituting for head coach Woody Hayes), a school administrator whom Cassady never met on the trip, Lou Berliner and Paul Horning of the *Columbus Dispatch*, Kay Kessler and Tom Keyes of the *Citizen*, and a reporter from the *Morning Journal*. When they arrived in New York, Strobel dropped Cassady off at the DAC, and then disappeared until the awards dinner.

Upon his arrival at the DAC, Cassady did several radio and television interviews, ate lunch, and then did more interviews. Since everything was all set up, and the time went so fast, he can't recall very much about the events surrounding the Heisman.

Cassady only owned a sport coat. As a result, one of the organizers of the event arranged to have a department store, Lazarus, donate a suit to Hop so he could wear it to the banquet that evening. The award's directors, Harold Reinauer and his father, did not organize the fete that the Heisman is today. None of Cassady's family were present, nor were there any other players in attendance. Only when Cassady returned to Columbus was a larger reception organized and attended by university and civic dignitaries.

Because the Heisman award ceremony was accompanied with relatively little fanfare, Hop did not return to the banquet until convinced by Rudy Riska to attend. As Cassady notes, "You can certainly tell the difference from then to when Rudy took over. He has done a great job! Everybody enjoys it and gets along with each other. Rudy made the Heisman Trophy a famous thing. It [the Heisman] gets bigger, bigger and bigger. The bigger it gets, the better it is."

Cassady notes that Rudy now makes it a point to bring in families and friends of perspective winners. "Some winners bring more guests today than there were people at my presentation," quips Cassady. Still, he feels the Heisman deserves its place at the head table. "The Heisman is still the fairest award because you have people from different regions vote on the winner. I hope whomever they get to take over Rudy's job approaches the award with the same enthusiasm and dedication as Rudy. He has made it a great award."

After a distinguished professional football career (in 1956, Cassady signed a contract for a $15,000 salary, plus a $15,000 contract which was more than Johnny Unitas made at the time), Cassady turned his attentions to his "other" favorite sport—baseball. He currently works as a baseball scout for the Yankees during the Big 10 season, and as a coach for the Yankees' farm club, the Columbus Clippers. For Cassady, the Heisman fraternity remains an integral part of his life. "When I'm not busy on the diamond, I try to see other Heisman winners, such as fellow Ohio State alum Archie Griffin, Les Horvath and Vic Janowicz at golf outings. It is always a great time."

—Hopalong Cassady

Pat Sullivan, Auburn, 1971

"I originally saw the announcement that I had won the 1971 Heisman on TV Thanksgiving night, during halftime of the Georgia-Georgia State game. What a great thrill. I remember arriving in New York City for the awards ceremony in December. One of the first things I recall is Rudy having to take me to get an overcoat, because being from the deep South I didn't have one.

"I stayed at the Downtown Athletic Club during my time in New York, and I really was in a trance… everything was going at such a fast pace. One thing that I remember is that John Wayne was the guest speaker the evening of the awards dinner and that Jim Plunkett and Pete Dawkins were present at the dinner. John Ott was president of the DAC at that time, and I won't ever forget the remarks he gave. He said: 'Welcome to the fraternity. It will mark you for the rest of your life.' Never has anyone been more correct.

"I look forward to seeing my wonderful friend Rudy each year. He is the common link that keeps the past Heisman winners together. The Heisman really does mark you. My family takes great pride in it, as well as my teammates, my coaches and the state of Alabama. I have subconsciously tried not to use or capitalize on the Heisman, but I will say that it gives you instant credibility in everything you do. It has been my privilege to be associated with the Heisman as part of the distinguished list of past winners."

—Pat Sullivan

1971 HEISMAN TROPHY WINNER PAT SULLIVAN

JOHN LATTNER, NOTRE DAME, 1953

"I won the award in 1953. Moose Krause called me on the phone and told me that I had just been named the Heisman Trophy winner. I was scheduled to go to New York City for four days. They asked if I would like to bring a girlfriend along, but I wasn't really seeing anyone too seriously at the time. As a result, I decided to bring my mother, Mae Lattner, to the festivities. She had never flown on a plane, much less been to New York, so it was a great thrill for her. She flew out of Chicago Midway, and I jumped on the plane in South Bend and off we went to New York.

"I believe my mother was the first woman to ever stay at the Downtown Athletic Club. When we got to New York, they had a limo waiting for us. After they picked us up, they asked my mother if there was anything she wanted to see. My mother wanted to see the big ships that were still popular back at that time—the Queen Mary and the Queen Elizabeth. She got a big kick out of seeing both ships. A fine gentleman by the name of Mr. Tierney was our host, and one evening we went out to all of the hot spots...the Stork Club, Leone's... five or six different places in all. We ended up at the Copacabana. Mom always loved a good martini, and the Copa didn't disappoint her. Although she had bad knees, which made it difficult for her to get around, my mother loved watching the dancing girls at the Copa. About 2 a.m., Mr. Tierney came up to me and mentioned that

1953 HEISMAN TROPHY WINNER JOHN LATTNER. JOHN WAS THE FOURTH NOTRE DAME PLAYER TO WIN THE AWARD. ALONG WITH HIS WIFE PEG, JOHN RETURNS EACH YEAR FOR THE HEISMAN FESTIVITIES.

tomorrow would be a long day, and that we would be on our feet most of the time, hinting that maybe we should get going. I told him to ask mom, who by this time, had had quite a few of those good Copa martinis. When Mr. Tierney mentioned to her that tomorrow would be a long day, again hinting that maybe we should get going, Mom looked at him and decided that instead of drinking another martini, she'd better have a Miller beer. To this day, the events of that night still make me chuckle. We ended up staying out until 4 a.m., and had quite a night to remember.

"Winning the Heisman Trophy has had a great impact on both my football and my professional career. After winning the Heisman in '53, I became targeted, in a way, by the pros. Since they didn't want to be shown up by a so-called Heisman hotshot, it was important to earn the respect of the players and management, because they were going to test you early on and see if you had what it took to be a player in the league. All factors considered, I think I was able to handle that situation, while at the same time, be somewhat of a draw that management could feature to get people to come out to the games because I was a Heisman winner.

"I don't think I felt the impact of receiving the award professionally until I started going back to the Heisman awards dinner in the 1970s, largely due to the urging of Rudy Riska. In my first year back, I attended the ceremony in which John Cappelletti received the Heisman. Television had really taken the Heisman to a new level, and it took the past winners right along for the ride.

"A number of us would be featured during the television awards show or our faces and names shown on the screen that was beamed across the country. This really had an impact on my sales career as the notoriety of being a Heisman Trophy winner opened up many doors that otherwise would have remained closed. Not surprisingly, the Heisman was always a great conversation piece whenever I was on a sales call.

"In addition, I kept the trophy on display at one of my restaurants. I always felt a great deal of pride whenever a father and son would come in just to get a glimpse or touch the trophy. It really makes me realize just how prestigious it is to be a Heisman Trophy winner.

"Rudy has always worked hard to put the Heisman and the past winners up another notch. He is always thinking of us first. Everything he does, he does first class. I truly enjoy coming back each year and seeing all of the great guys and being part of the enthusiasm surrounding the Heisman, from Rudy to all of the people who attend the banquet. I don't know how many more trips out to New York I have left in me, but if Rudy calls, you can count on John Lattner being there."

—John Lattner

Gary Beban, UCLA, 1967

"As the Downtown Athletic Club exists as the home of the Heisman Trophy, Rudy Riska voluntarily serves as the spirit and caretaker of the bronze figure. He is the personal connection for the recipients, who span decades of college football history and generations, as 65 years have passed from the first to the most recent winner. The game and Rudy's loving friendship, through sport, glory, and life tensions, is the most common thread

Heisman Trophy winners possess. He unifies a very diverse team of individuals and history.

"My first visit to New York City in 1967 was my introduction to the Trophy and Rudy Riska. I do not separate the importance or the significance of the events. At the time, it was the longest trip my father and I had ever taken together; my mom was too shy and nervous to join us. It was also the first time the Beban boys donned tuxedoes, and mom wasn't at our side to help us. My father was married in his Navy uniform, so it was all new to him.

"Heisman week and the surrounding ceremonies involved a menu of contrasts. Bundled in his Navy pea coat, my father explained to me his perceived experience of my mother entering this country as a child through Ellis Island. At the same time, I tried to rationalize to him the Vietnam protesters who were marching in the alleys of Wall Street. While viewing the pictures of the former winners posted on a wall, he whispered, in a respectful manner, their stories to me. Together, in the same room, we would endure the blasting rhetoric of a Howard Cosell interview. As UCLA football coach Tom Prothro and UCLA Athletic Director JD Morgan reflected on game and career successes, I realized college memories, which seemed so fresh just a moment ago, would soon be fading memories.

"Through it all, there was a consistent smile, a supporting handshake, and a hand on my shoulder, guiding me through crowds of friendly strangers; it was Rudy. Frank Eliscu produced it, the Downtown Athletic Club and the sportswriters award it, and fortunate collegiate participants receive it. But, the Heisman Trophy's Most Valuable Player is Rudy Riska. It is Rudy's life-long genuineness, without any favors requested in return, that separates the uniqueness of the Heisman Trophy from all the other awards that carry my name."

—Gary Beban

1967 HEISMAN TROPHY WINNER GARY BEBAN WITH DAC PRESIDENT JOE MCGOLDRICK, AS PAUL HORNUNG LOOKS ON.

129

JOHN CAPPELLETTI, PENN STATE, 1973

"When it was announced that I had won the Heisman Trophy, I was in the middle of taping the Bob Hope College All-American Football Special. As soon as we were finished taping, I was transported to the Downtown Athletic Club in the back of a stretch limo with Bob Hope as the only other passenger. Not surprisingly, from the minute I won the Heisman, special things started to happen.

"At that time, I was the only player from Penn State to win the Heisman, so I knew how excited and proud everyone at the University must have been. But most importantly, my family was able to celebrate and enjoy this event at a time when my youngest brother was ill with leukemia, and we all needed something to lift our spirits.

"Meeting and getting to know the former Heisman Trophy winners, the members and staff at the Downtown Athletic Club, and numerous other sports celebrities was certainly special. It was a day I will always remember.

"One memory of that day that will always stand out above the rest was meeting Rudy Riska. From the moment I stepped into the Downtown Athletic Club, he made my family and me feel welcome. He knew how hectic the next 72 hours would be for me and how confusing it might be for my family. Rudy took care of every detail, and the weekend activities couldn't have gone any better.

JOHN CAPPELLETTI WITH HIS PARENTS
AND YOUNGER BROTHER JOEY.

"Rudy not only cares for the individual Heisman winners, such as myself, year-after-year, but he has cared for and held dear the Heisman Trophy and what it represents, for many years. If I had to pick one individual that has all the characteristics you would want to see in a Heisman Trophy winner, it would be Rudy Riska."

—*John Cappelletti*

ANGELO BERTELLI, NOTRE DAME, 1943 & THE ATOM BOWL

Angelo Bertelli, the Notre Dame standout quarterback won the Heisman Trophy in 1943. However, absent from most accounts of the "Springfield Rifle's" storied Irish career was a game played at a site indelibly inked in U.S. history and far from the football field at South Bend.

Like many collegiate football stars, Bertelli was a member of the U.S. Armed Forces, more specifically, a Lieutenant in the United States Marine Corps Second Marine Division. The game in question pitted two rival units from this division. That former collegiate and professional football players met up to stage a game was an unremarkable occurrence (lest the reader forget the hilarious football scene depicted in the movie *MASH*.) What made this game special, however, was its location—Nagasaki, Japan.

1943 HEISMAN TROPHY WINNER ANGELO BERTELLI WITH DAC PRESIDENT JOE TAYLOR AND LEGENDARY NOTRE DAME COACH FRANK LEAHY.

On August 9th, 1945 at 11:02 a.m., a U.S. B-29 dropped a 22-kiloton fission bomb, nicknamed "Fat Man," on the Japanese city of Nagasaki, wiping the 1.8 square miles of city from the map. In the aftermath, the Second Marines were sent into the decimated city six weeks later.

The two teams, Bertelli's Nagasaki Bears, and the Isahaya Tigers (captained by "Bullet" Bill Osmanski, the former Holy Cross Crusader and Chicago Bear fullback) needed to find a suitable place to stage the game.* Pre-war topographers would have told you that Nagasaki was located in the hilly Urakami River Valley, but the effects of the atomic blast created a suitable playing surface for football. The name of the field was "Atomic Athletic Field # 2." Bertelli and Osmanski began recruiting former players to take part in the game. When they were finished, they had players such as Randall Stallings of Arkansas, Pat Preston of Wake Forest, Phil Conrad of Washington, W.C. Johnson and H. Bollier of Northwest Louisiana, Steve Stevens of Michigan State, Gorham "Stan" Getchell of Temple, and Ted Bukowski of Duquesne, to name just a few of the former athletes who agreed to participate in the game. The game was slated for New Year's Day, 1946, less than four months after the nuclear blast that leveled Nagasaki. So, while Americans were gearing up to watch their favorite bowl games, Bertelli and company prepared to take part in the "Atom Bowl."

Bertelli and Osmanski adopted special rules for the game. As listed in the game's program, "Professional Football League rules will apply, with the following exceptions: a) two-handed touch instead of tackle; b) fifteen yards for a first down." The former rule was a result of the effects of the bombing that resulted in the field being littered with broken glass. A final rule was agreed upon to keep the peace between the two units during their stay in Japan. Both Bertelli and Osmanski agreed to have the game end in a tie. This secret was carried to the grave of all the players, save Bertelli.

The Bears jumped out to a 13-0 first half lead on the strength of two Bertelli scoring passes. However, in the second half, Osmanski ran in for two scores, creating a 13-13 tie as the final seconds ticked away. Fully expecting Osmanski to adhere to the agreement about ending the game in a tie, Bertelli was stunned as Osmanski's PAT sailed through the uprights, giving the Tigers a 14-13 victory. Then, Osmanski turned to Bertelli and flashed a grin, letting the Heisman winner know that all was fair in football and war.

* Information about this game was taken with the author's permission from John D. Lukac's article, *"The Atom Bowl"*, that originally was published in the 2000 pre-season edition of the *Athlon* magazine.

"LEAHY'S LADS"

"Notre Dame, with seven Heisman Trophy winners and its rich history and football traditions, has been an important ingredient to the Heisman Trophy. We have been fortunate in recent years to become part of the 'Leahy's Lads' group, comprised of some of college football's great players, and more important, great people.

Jack Connor, who authored a book on the legendary coach Frank Leahy and those great teams and players, along with Jerry Groom, the former Notre Dame All-American and College Hall-of-Famer, lead the way in keeping the memory of Coach Leahy alive. They head up the Frank Leahy Scholarship Program, as well as being instrumental in the creation of the statue of Coach Leahy outside of Notre Dame stadium.

It has been an honor to participate in the year-round programs that serve as an inspiration for all."

—Rudy Riska

STEVE OWENS, OKLAHOMA, 1969

"1969 was a special year—man went to the moon; the New York Mets and the New York Jets won world championships; Woodstock was a watershed event; and Dave Thomas opened his first Wendy's restaurant. It was also a very special year for me and my family. I was awarded the Heisman Memorial Trophy and met my dear friend, Rudy Riska.

"I was born and raised in small towns in Oklahoma, one of nine children, and I was overwhelmed with the thought of going to New York City in the first place, let alone to receive an award of such honor. My mom and dad had never even been on an airplane before that trip, and I could sense their anxiety. Thank goodness my wife, Barbara, was the one who kept us all grounded as we prepared to travel to the Big Apple.

"Finally, the day arrived, and with much anticipation and excitement, we left Oklahoma for the bright lights of NYC. The first person I met was Rudy Riska. He was warm, friendly, helpful and kind. He immediately made all of us feel at ease and genuinely welcome. I sensed even then that I had made a lifelong friend.

AS HIS WIFE, BARBARA, LOOKS ON, 1969 HEISMAN WINNER STEVE OWENS PRESENTS A PAIR OF DAC CUFFLINKS TO PRESIDENT RICHARD NIXON.

"Over the last thirty-plus years, Rudy has become a member of the Owens' extended family. Our treasured friendship has endured and strengthened with time, and we feel blessed to have Rudy in our lives.

"When I think of the Heisman Trophy, I, of course, think of my University of Oklahoma teammates and coaches. But, what first comes to mind is Rudy Riska. Rudy exemplifies the Heisman award and what it stands for. Rudy is the glue that keeps the Heisman family together. "Yes, 1969 was a very special year. Rudy Riska became a part of my life forever."

—Steve Owens

ARCHIE GRIFFIN, OHIO STATE, 1974 & 1975

"I really had no idea that I would win the Heisman as a junior in 1974. I knew I was a candidate that year because I had finished 5th in the Heisman voting the previous year (a year when Ohio State had three of the top six vote getters). I found out from our sports information staff, Director Marv Homan and his assistant Steve Snapp, that I was one of three players that would be invited to New York City and the Downtown Athletic Club. I was told that a Heisman representative would escort me to New York for the announcement on a Tuesday. The escort turned out to be Irv Cross.

"When we arrived in New York City (which was my first time in the Big Apple), a limousine was waiting to take us to the DAC. Everything was first class. As we were waiting at the DAC for the time when the announcement of the winner would be made, I realized that I was the only player invited. At that point, I thought I had a pretty good chance of winning!

TWO-TIME HEISMAN TROPHY WINNER ARCHIE GRIFFIN WITH BOB HOPE
ON THE BOB HOPE ALL-AMERICAN TELEVISION SHOW.

"After the announcement was made, I flew back to Columbus, Ohio, Tuesday evening so I could be at practice Wednesday, since the Ohio State team was preparing for the Rose Bowl. Coach Woody Hayes was extremely proud that "we" had won the award. "We" meant the team. He was right because without my teammates, and in particular the offensive line, I would not have had a chance at the Heisman.

"Arrangements were made for my family to join me in New York for the Heisman festivities. Malcolm and Valentine McCloud were my host family for the weekend and really made me feel at home. The pre-Heisman dinner on Sunday evening was a very special event, because many of the past winners attended. I was told that the year before, John Cappelletti had made a tremendous speech and that it could get emotional for me Monday evening at the Heisman dinner held at the Hilton. Sure enough, I didn't get ten words into my speech Monday night when I started crying! When I returned to Ohio State on Tuesday, my teammates let me have it for crying on national TV.

"The following year in 1975, I was going to a speaking engagement in Bel Air, Ohio the day the DAC was to announce the three Heisman finalists. Assistant Sports Information Director Steve Snapp asked that I check in with him from the road. Prior to the speaking engagement, I gave Steve a call and, sure enough, I had been invited to the DAC. Recalling my 1974 experience, my invitation meant I had become the first player in history to win back-to-back Heisman Trophies. Steve admitted as much, but asked that I not tell anyone until the DAC made the official announcement nationally the next day.

"In 1975, I not only brought my family out to New York for the awards dinner, but also Ohio State assistant coach Keith Jackson, Coach Hayes and the captains of the '75 team: Cornelius Green, Tim Fox, Brian Baschnagel and Ken Kuhn. It meant a lot to me to have those guys in attendance, because we all came into school together and as a group, graduated as a very successful class at Ohio State. I did have to promise not to cry during my speech! Again, the hospitality that was shown to us by Rudy Riska and the DAC staff was incredible.

"I feel fortunate to be a two-time winner of the Heisman. I think there will be another two-time winner in the future. It will most likely be a player who wins for the first time as a freshman or sophomore, because most guys that win the Heisman as juniors leave college for the NFL.

"I also feel fortunate that I am included in the fraternity of Heisman winners. I have always enjoyed getting together with the past winners, particularly the other Ohio State winners—Vic Janowicz, Hopalong Cassady, Les Horvath and Eddie George. It is true that you are linked forever with the award. I will always be introduced as two-time Heisman winner Archie Griffin, and that is very humbling. The Heisman has allowed me to go and do things that would never have been available to me otherwise. Whether it is a speaking engagement, travel or invitations to different functions, the Heisman has provided many wonderful opportunities for me. One of those wonderful opportunities is being able to be a part of the Wendy's High School Heisman program, an exceptional program that was started through the efforts of Dave Thomas. I am proud to be a part of that program because it recognizes kids doing great things in their lives, not just one aspect of life. The kids getting recognized might be great athletes, but they are also great students and people."

—Archie Griffin

"The world has been a better place to live in because of Rudy Riska. My life has been fuller because of my association with Rudy and the great Heisman winners. Thank you for being my friend, Rudy."

—Jay Berwanger
1935 Heisman Trophy Winner

"Rudy has given of his time freely for many charity functions and his warmth and gentleness brightens any affair he attends. He has always been a friend to the Heisman winners, but it's well known he becomes friends with everyone he meets."

—John Lujack
1947 Heisman Trophy Winner

"Rudy has always worked hard to put the Heisman Trophy and the past winners up another notch. I truly enjoy coming back each year and seeing all of the great guys and being part of the enthusiasm surrounding the Heisman. I don't know how many more trips out to New York I have left in me, but if Rudy calls, you can count on John Lattner being there."

—John Lattner
1953 Heisman Trophy Winner

"There is a reason that I have only missed one Heisman ceremony since 1966—Rudy Riska. Rudy is a friend to all of the former Heisman winners, and he truly does a great job of keeping the fraternity of Heisman winners together. I am proud to call him my friend."

—Steve Spurrier
Head Coach, University of Florida
1966 Heisman Trophy Winner

"Frank Eliscu produced it, the Downtown Athletic Club and sportswriters award it, and fortunate collegiate participants receive it, but the Heisman Trophy's Most Valuable Player is Rudy Riska."

—Gary Beban
1967 Heisman Trophy Winner

"Rudy not only cares for the individual Heisman winners, such as myself, year after year, but he has cared for and held dear the Heisman Trophy and what it represents, for many years. If I had to pick one individual that has all the characteristics you would want to see in a Heisman Trophy winner, it would be Rudy Riska."

—John Cappelletti
1973 Heisman Trophy Winner

"When I think back to the two years that I attended the Heisman banquet and reflect on my experiences in New York, I have very few memories that do not include Rudy Riska. For myself, the Heisman award, its tradition, its prestige, and all that it has come to be is synonymous with Rudy Riska."

—Danny Wuerffel
1996 Heisman Trophy Winner